GCSE Science
CORE HIGHER REVISION BOOK

Mike Boyle, Philip Dobson
and Steve Witney

Hodder Murray

A MEMBER OF THE HODDER HEADLINE GROUP

Acknowledgements

Every effort has been made to trace all copyright holders, but if any have been inadvertently overlooked the Publishers will be pleased to make the necessary arrangements at the first opportunity.

Although every effort has been made to ensure that website addresses are correct at time of going to press, Hodder Murray cannot be held responsible for the content of any website mentioned in this book. It is sometimes possible to find a relocated web page by typing in the address of the home page for a website in the URL window of your browser.

Hodder Headline's policy is to use papers that are natural, renewable and recyclable products and made from wood grown in sustainable forests. The logging and manufacturing processes are expected to conform to the environmental regulations of the country of origin.

Orders: please contact Bookpoint Ltd, 130 Milton Park, Abingdon, Oxon OX14 4SB. Telephone: (44) 01235 827720. Fax: (44) 01235 400454. Lines are open 9.00–17.00, Monday to Saturday, with a 24-hour message answering service. Visit our website at www.hoddereducation.co.uk

© Mike Boyle, Philip Dobson, Steve Witney 2007
First published in 2007 by
Hodder Murray, an imprint of Hodder Education,
a member of the Hodder Headline Group
338 Euston Road
London NW1 3BH

Impression number   5 4 3 2 1
Year   2011 2010 2009 2008 2007

Cover photos Science Photo Library: dragonfly, Andy Harmer; house, Ted Kinsman; limestone, Alfred Pasieka
Illustrations by Barking Dog Art
Typeset in Times New Roman 11.5pt by Fakenham Photosetting Ltd, Fakenham Norfolk
Printed in Italy

A catalogue record for this title is available from the British Library

ISBN-13: 978 0340 91422 9

Contents

Nervous system and reflexes

The nervous system

1 The nervous system allows you to **detect** what's going on both inside and outside your body, and to **respond** in the right way.
2 It does this by detecting **stimuli** and sending this information into your **central nervous system (CNS)**, which is your **brain and spinal cord**.
3 A **stimulus** is a change in the environment that we can detect, such as light, sound, movement, heat, etc.
4 **Receptors** are cells that can detect a particular stimulus. **Sense organs**, like the eye, ear and skin, contain a lot of these receptor cells.
5 Receptor cells send this information along specialised cells called **neurones**, or **nerve cells**, which are like tiny wires.
6 Most of this sensory information goes to our **brain**, which **processes** the information and **coordinates** a response, often based on memory. For instance, we may see somebody, recognise them, and call out their name.
7 The organ that makes the response is called the **effector**. This could be a muscle or a gland that responds by releasing a chemical, such as a hormone.

The senses

There are five senses. They are:

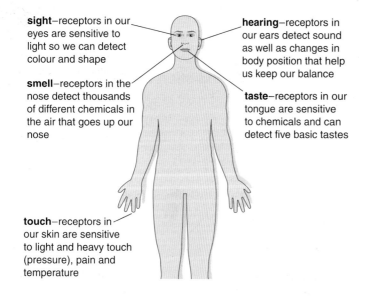

sight—receptors in our eyes are sensitive to light so we can detect colour and shape

smell—receptors in the nose detect thousands of different chemicals in the air that goes up our nose

touch—receptors in our skin are sensitive to light and heavy touch (pressure), pain and temperature

hearing—receptors in our ears detect sound as well as changes in body position that help us keep our balance

taste—receptors in our tongue are sensitive to chemicals and can detect five basic tastes

A single neurone or nerve cell

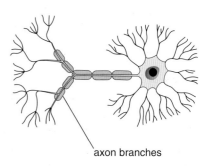

axon branches

■ Neurones (or nerve cells) can be very long and transmit information from one part of the body to another

exam tip

★ Many exam answers confuse sense organs with receptors – 'the skin is a receptor' would get no marks. The skin is a sense organ that contains many different receptor cells.

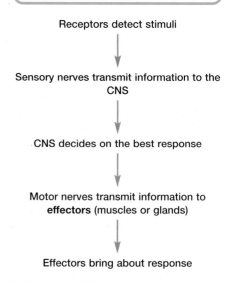

Receptors detect stimuli

↓

Sensory nerves transmit information to the CNS

↓

CNS decides on the best response

↓

Motor nerves transmit information to **effectors** (muscles or glands)

↓

Effectors bring about response

■ Overview of the nervous system

Reflexes

A **reflex** is a quick response. There are many different reflexes, often designed to protect us from danger, or to keep our balance and body position. Examples of reflexes include:

- blinking when something comes near to your eye;
- jerking your hand away from a hot or sharp object;
- the knee jerk (when tapped just under the kneecap).

The key features of reflexes are:

- they are fast;
- they are automatic – they do not involve the conscious control of the brain, so you can't stop them, even if you wanted to;
- the **same stimulus** always leads to the **same response**;
- they don't involve many neurones – the diagram shows that just three neurones are involved: sensory, relay and motor.

exam tip

★ Always talk about nerve **impulses**, not messages. A nerve impulse carries information, but it's the brain's job to make sense of the tiny electrical blips and 'decode' the message.

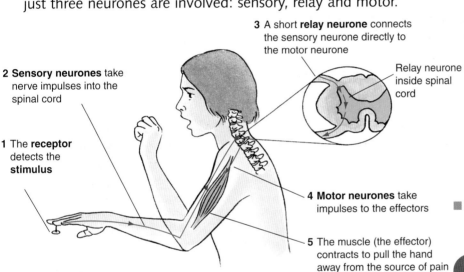

2 **Sensory neurones** take nerve impulses into the spinal cord

3 A short **relay neurone** connects the sensory neurone directly to the motor neurone

Relay neurone inside spinal cord

1 The **receptor** detects the **stimulus**

4 **Motor neurones** take impulses to the effectors

5 The muscle (the effector) contracts to pull the hand away from the source of pain

■ The basic components of a reflex action

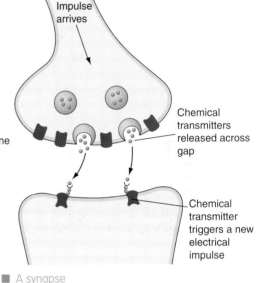

Impulse arrives

Chemical transmitters released across gap

Chemical transmitter triggers a new electrical impulse

■ A synapse

Synapses

1 A **synapse** is a junction between two neurones, such as between a relay neurone and a sensory neurone in a reflex action.
2 When a nerve impulse reaches a synapse, a **transmitter chemical** is released. This passes (diffuses) across the gap and sets up an impulse in the next neurone.

check your understanding

❶ a) List seven different stimuli that you can detect. *(7 marks)*
b) State two differences between sensory and motor nerves. *(2 marks)*

check your understanding

❷ Match the words A–E to numbers 1–5 in the paragraph. *(5 marks)*

A effectors   B motor nerves   C sense organ   D sensory nerves   E receptor cells

The eye is an example of a ____1____ that contains millions of ____2____, which are sensitive to light. The information they gather passes along ____3____ to the brain. The brain processes this information and coordinates a response. Impulses pass along ____4____ to the ____5____, which could be the muscles of the chest, throat and tongue that allow us to speak.

Hormones, the menstrual cycle and fertility

Hormones are chemical signals

1 **Hormones** are compounds made and secreted by **glands** such as the ovaries, testes and pituitary gland.
2 Hormones always travel in the blood.
3 They have an effect on **target cells**. These cells may be in one particular organ, or scattered throughout the body.

The menstrual cycle

The menstrual cycle is a woman's monthly reproductive cycle. Every month an egg, or **ovum**, is developed in one of the **ovaries** and then released, in a process called **ovulation**.

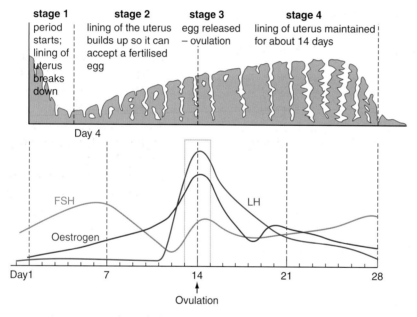

■ The changes in the uterus lining, levels of oestrogen, LH and FSH during an average 28-day menstrual cycle

> ### exam tip
>
> **Adrenaline – a very fast acting hormone**
>
> You are not expected to know about adrenaline, but if you were told in an exam question that when your body releases adrenaline:
>
> ★ your heart beats faster;
> ★ you breathe more deeply;
> ★ blood is redirected to your muscles from your skin and intestines (producing the feeling of 'butterflies'),
>
> then you would be able to state that the target cells for the adrenaline are in the heart, breathing muscles, skin and intestine.

There are three hormones involved – **FSH**, **oestrogen** and **LH**.

Hormone	Full name	Where it's made	What it does	When
FSH	Follicle-stimulating hormone	Pituitary gland	1 Stimulates the development of an egg inside a follicle 2 Stimulates the ovary to release oestrogen	Day 1 (when the period starts) to about day 13
Oestrogen	Oestrogen	Ovary	1 Causes uterus lining to thicken 2 Inhibits production of more FSH 3 Stimulates the pituitary gland to produce LH	Day 5 (after period) to day 28 About day 12–13 Day 13–14
LH	Luteinising hormone	Pituitary gland	Causes ovulation	About day 14

Hormones can be used to control fertility

As hormones control the development of eggs and ovulation, we can use hormones as **contraceptives**, and we can also use them in **fertility treatment** to help couples to conceive a baby.

1 The contraceptive pill ('**the pill**') contains oestrogen. High levels of oestrogen inhibit the production of FSH. No FSH, no egg develops, no ovulation, no baby.
2 A common cause of **infertility** is **low levels of FSH**, so that eggs do not mature and cannot be released. Treatment involves taking FSH to **stimulate egg production**.

The pill has advantages and disadvantages:

- it is very **effective** – 99% of women on the pill do not get pregnant – but some do;
- it may make periods lighter and less painful;
- it gives no protection against sexually transmitted diseases, such as HIV and chlamydia;
- it may have **side effects**, such as headaches, nausea, irregular periods and water retention.

In **IVF** (**in vitro fertilisation**, where 'in vitro' means 'in glass'), the woman is given FSH so that her ovaries produce more eggs than normal, and LH to stimulate the release of these eggs. The eggs are collected and fertilised by sperm *in vitro*. The fertilised eggs develop into embryos and are implanted.

Risks and problems of fertility treatment:

- it may not work, and trying again and again may be time-consuming, stressful and expensive;
- it may result in over-stimulation of the ovaries, resulting in **multiple births**, triplets, quads, etc.

exam tip

★ Make sure you can list the ethical issues, as well as the benefits and risks of IVF. Many people object to IVF on the grounds that an embryo is a human being, with rights, from the moment of conception. IVF creates many embryos that will never be used, and this could be seen as a waste of human life.

check your understanding

❸ Match the words A–D to the numbers 1–4 in the paragraph. *(4 marks)*

   A ovaries   B oestrogen   C luteinising hormone   D pituitary

Puberty in girls begins when the ___1___ gland begins to secrete the hormone FSH. The target organs of this hormone are the ___2___. In turn, this gland secretes the hormone ___3___. Rising levels of this hormone stimulate the pituitary gland to release the hormone ___4___, which causes ovulation.

❹ a) At what point in the menstrual cycle is a woman at her most fertile? *(1 mark)*
   b) A simple blood test can be used to diagnose hormone deficiencies. Explain why a blood test for low hormone levels must be done at a certain time of the month. *(2 marks)*

Controlling internal conditions

Homeostasis means 'keeping constant internal conditions' – while your outside environment may change, the conditions inside your body stay remarkably constant. It's all about keeping your cells bathed in just the right conditions so that they can work efficiently.

Conditions that need to be controlled include:

- water content – we don't want to become dehydrated or over-hydrated;
- ion content (think of it as 'salt balance');
- temperature – enzymes in cells work most efficiently at about 37 °C;
- blood sugar (glucose) levels, in order to provide cells with energy.

Important ions include sodium, chloride (sodium chloride = common table salt), potassium and calcium. These ions are sometimes called **electrolytes**.

Glucose in the blood must be kept within certain limits. People who cannot control their blood glucose levels are **diabetic**.

We can lose water in several ways:

- in sweat;
- in urine;
- in our breath;
- in faeces (we lose a lot more water when we have diarrhoea).

This water loss, and ions lost in sweat, must be replaced from our food and drink. People who sweat more need more water and more salt – but many of us have too much salt in our diet.

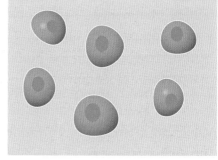

■ All the cells in your body are surrounded by tissue fluid, from which they get all their nutrients and oxygen. They also excrete their waste into it. It is the job of our circulation to keep this tissue fluid 'fresh' – a vital aspect of homeostasis

● Homeostasis, the nervous system and hormones

1 Body temperature is controlled by a combination of temperature receptors and effectors.
2 Your brain can detect the temperature of the blood flowing though it, and make responses that increase or decrease body temperature as needed e.g. sweating or shivering.
3 Specialised cells in the **pancreas** act as both receptors and effectors, so they can detect and control changes in blood glucose levels.

Receptor cells in the pancreas detect increased or decreased levels of glucose, and respond by making and secreting the hormones insulin and glucagon. These hormones circulate in the blood, and act on cells to make them take in or release more glucose until the level in the blood is back to normal.

Evaluating sports drinks

When we exercise our muscles we use glucose as a source of energy, and we sweat to keep cool. So when we are active we lose glucose, salt and water, all of which need to be replaced.

Isotonic drinks have the same concentration of dissolved substances as our blood and body fluids.

Imagine you are investigating the claim:

> 'Our isotonic drink keeps you going for 33% longer'

What information would you need in order to convince you that this was a **valid** and **reliable** claim? You could ask the manufacturers for their **evidence**, or you could design your own **investigation** to see if the findings can be repeated.

Some questions you might like to ask are:

1 '33% longer' is a comparison. Longer than what? What would you measure it against – what would be your **control**?
2 is the manufacturer's claim a **valid** way of comparing how good the sports drink is, or could **other factors** affect the athlete's performance?
3 how many athletes were in your sample? There needs to be a large enough sample to make the investigation **reliable**.
4 how did you choose your sample of athletes? Was there any **bias**?
5 how many times was the experiment repeated? Is that enough data to make your investigation **reliable**?
6 could you get the same effect from simply drinking water with a little salt and glucose dissolved in it?

■ Isotonic drinks are designed to replace the ions we lose – so do they taste like sweat?

check your understanding

⑤ If you have been exercising, you will have lost water and start to become dehydrated.
  a) State two ways that exercise may increase water output. *(2 marks)*
  b) Give a reason why you should eat or drink fluids containing both water **and** ions. *(1 mark)*
  c) Give an example of one other circumstance in which the body may need to replace both water and ions. *(1 mark)*

⑥ Which of the following are **not** controlled by internal mechanisms in the body? *(1 mark)*

  A temperature   B energy intake
  C water output of the body   D ion concentration in cells

exam tip

★ When we say that data are **reliable**, it means the data can be trusted because other measurements (by another person, or another technique) have given the same result.

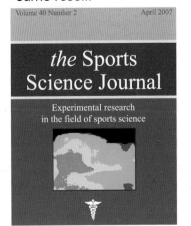

Volume 40 Number 2   April 2007

the Sports Science Journal

Experimental research in the field of sports science

Drugs: good and bad

Drugs are compounds that affect your body's chemistry in some way. There are two types of drugs.

1 **Medical drugs** are medicines that are designed to treat a particular illness or condition. These drugs can still be used illegally, and can harm the body.
2 **Recreational drugs**, taken for their short-term effects. Many recreational drugs, such as cocaine, heroin and LSD, are illegal. However, the two drugs with the greatest effect on the nation's health, tobacco and alcohol, are legal if you are old enough.

● Why do people take recreational drugs?

It could be because people like their **short-term effects**:

- relaxation;
- stress relief – an escape from everyday worries;
- stimulation – some drugs (e.g. amphetamines or 'speed') combat tiredness so that people can work longer or 'party all night';
- inspiration – some people claim they are more creative while under the influence of drugs;
- pain relief – many multiple sclerosis sufferers claim that cannabis gives relief from muscular pain.

However, these drugs can lead to serious problems such as **addiction.** Heroin and cocaine are highly addictive. Alcohol and cigarettes are also addictive, and users can suffer **withdrawal symptoms** if they try to give up. **Brain damage** and **liver damage** are also consequences of drug abuse.

Alcohol is legal but dangerous. Alcohol reduces the activity of the nervous system, leading to:

- slower brain function;
- **slower reactions**, and **impaired coordination** and **judgement**, which is why it is illegal to drink and drive;
- loss of **self-control**, so people do things they wouldn't do when sober, such as saying 'yes' to sex.

Excess alcohol in one session – binge drinking – can cause **dehydration** (the main cause of hangovers), **unconsciousness** and even a **coma**.

Long-term alcohol abuse can result in liver damage (**cirrhosis**) and **brain damage**.

Because so many people drink alcohol, the cost of dealing with alcohol-related health problems (millions of working days lost), accidents caused by drink-drivers, and the **social costs** to families can be very high.

Testing and trialling medical drugs

Medical drugs have to undergo a long series of tests to make sure that they work and are safe to use.

Thalidomide – a drug that wasn't properly tested. In the 1950s, thalidomide was trialled as a sleeping pill or sedative. During the trials it was also found to be very effective against **morning sickness**, so it was also prescribed to **pregnant women**. The drug had not been tested on pregnant women.

Disastrously, the drug affected the **development of the fetus**, so that many children were born with very short and deformed arms or legs. Not surprisingly, the drug was banned in 1962 and more rigorous testing procedures, like those outlined on the right, were developed for new drugs.

'Not tested on animals'. Testing on animals is controversial because it may involve suffering and pain. You need to be able to offer opinions on both sides of the argument. For example:

Against	For
Testing drugs on animals is morally wrong because the animals suffer	The suffering of animals is unfortunate, but is insignificant compared with the benefits – the lives of many humans and animals are made better by the medicines that are proved to be safe
Drugs don't need to be tested on cats, dogs and monkeys – scientists could use animals that have no sense of pain, such as jellyfish or cockroaches	These animals are so different from mammals that the results would not be **valid**. Tests are needed on mammals

1 Natural substances are tested. Many plants are used by native peoples as traditional medicines or poisons. These and other species of plants or fungi can be tested to see if they contain substances that may be useful; for example, new painkillers or antibiotics.

2 **Laboratory tests** on human tissue samples. Sometimes this gives good results, but it can't show the effects on the whole body. For instance, you can't test the effectiveness of a sleeping pill on a sample of tissue.

3 Test the drug for toxicity and effectiveness **on live animals**. This gives more information because it uses a whole organism, but it usually has to be a mammal because humans are mammals.

4 **Clinical trials** – the drugs are tested on human volunteers to see if they are effective and if there are any **side effects**. The trials start with a low dose.

■ How new drugs are developed

check your understanding

❼ Match the words A–D to numbers 1–4 in the paragraph. *(4 marks)*

    A clinical trials   B human tissue   C side effects   D live animals

A promising new antibiotic has been found in a plant from the Amazon rainforest. The drug kills a wide variety of bacteria, but it must be tested to make sure that it has no _____1_____. Firstly, the drug is tested on samples of _____2_____. Then it is tested on whole organisms, which involves using _____3_____ to check for toxicity. Finally, the drug is tested in _____4_____.

❽ Imagine there is a hormone, produced by the brain, that makes you feel happy. It is an important part of homeostasis to keep the levels of this hormone more-or-less constant. If there is too little in the blood, the brain will make some more. If there is too much, the brain will stop production for a while. A drug becomes available that has the same effect as this hormone.

    a) What will the drug-user feel in the short term? *(1 mark)*
    b) Explain how the brain will respond to the high levels of this drug *(1 mark)*
    c) What will the drug-user feel after the effects of the drug have worn off? *(1 mark)*
    d) What does addiction mean? *(1 mark)*
    e) Use this information to explain how people can become addicted to a drug. *(1 mark)*

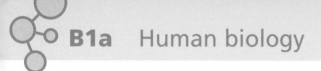

Tobacco and cannabis

Tobacco is legal in the UK for over-16s, while cannabis is illegal. Some people want to make cannabis legal, but this is controversial.

● What's in tobacco smoke?

- **Nicotine** – this relaxes smokers. It is not particularly dangerous, but it is **highly addictive**.
- **Tar** – a complex mixture of compounds, many of which are **carcinogenic** (cancer-causing).
- **Carbon monoxide** – a gas that sticks to haemoglobin, preventing the blood from carrying as much oxygen as it should. If pregnant women smoke, the fetus can be born underweight.

● There is a well established link between smoking and lung cancer

There is a **direct causal link** between **smoking** and **lung cancer**, which in plain English means that smoking causes lung cancer. Cancer Research UK estimates that 90% of lung cancer cases are due to smoking.

However, you can **never prove** that an individual smoker's lung cancer was caused by smoking; we can only say that it is **highly probable**.

● Evaluating ways to stop smoking

If you were asked to compare methods to see which is best, you could listen to someone's **opinion**, but that would not be very **reliable**. It would be based on a sample of one or a few people.

You could see what the manufacturers of nicotine patches claim, but their claims might be biased, and their evidence may not be **credible** because it wasn't gathered scientifically (see isotonic drinks on page 7).

You could **evaluate** effectiveness by looking at the data and seeing if there is a pattern. Remember to think about:

- Is the **sample size** large enough?
- Is the method **valid** – comparing only one factor?
- Could there be **other factors**, such as age, gender, diet or workplace environment, that the survey didn't take into account?

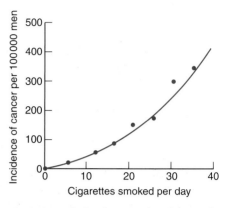

■ The **correlation** between smoking and deaths from lung cancer was noticed in the 1940s, but smoking as a **cause** was not accepted until more **evidence** came from interviews with many lung cancer patients. The **statistics** showed that nearly all were heavy smokers

What is cannabis?

Cannabis is a plant, the leaves of which are dried and smoked, producing a feeling of relaxation and mellowness. Many people think it is relatively harmless – but it is still **illegal**.

Objections to cannabis include:

- Many studies have linked cannabis use with an increased incidence of **mental illness**, such as **schizophrenia** – this could be due to chemicals in cannabis that affect the brain.
- People say cannabis could be a 'gateway drug' to harder, more addictive drugs – there is some evidence that most users of hard drugs have tried cannabis first.

If you were asked to evaluate the **link between cannabis and hard drugs** you would need to use the information provided to consider the evidence for and against. Be careful to separate **opinions** influenced by social and moral judgements from **evidence**, such as long-term studies on large groups of people, including a control group.

check your understanding

⑨ Emma, a heavy smoker who does not want to give up, says 'Mr Smith up the road died from lung cancer, and he never smoked one cigarette in his life.'

Which statement below, about the link between smoking and lung cancer, explains why Emma has a higher risk of getting lung cancer than Mr Smith? *(1 mark)*

A Smoking does not cause lung cancer.
B Not all smokers get lung cancer.
C Passive smoking can cause lung cancer.
D Most people who die from lung cancer are heavy smokers.

⑩ In the UK in 2004–05, 26% of men and 23% of women were cigarette smokers, compared with the early 1970s, when around 50% of men and 40% of women smoked.
a) Explain why it can be difficult to give up smoking. *(2 marks)*

Deaths due to lung cancer have fallen even more dramatically than the number of smokers since the 1970s.
b) Apart from the drop in the number of smokers, suggest why the numbers of people dying from lung cancer have fallen. *(2 marks)*
c) State one other advantage for women of stopping smoking. *(1 mark)*

⑪ A scientist notices that the incidence of skin cancer is highest in the areas of highest ice cream sales. Explain why it is wrong to claim that ice cream causes skin cancer. *(3 marks)*

Diet and exercise

The statement 'you are what you eat' is true – our bodies are made up from the food we have eaten. However, if our food contains more energy than we use, we will store the extra as fat, and this can be a big problem.

● Balanced diet – the right amount of energy and a balance of different nutrients

- **Carbohydrates** (such as sugars and starch) for energy.
- **Fats** to provide **insulation** and to make cells.
- **Proteins** for growth, cell repair and cell replacement.
- Small amounts of **minerals** and **vitamins** for various chemical reactions in the body.
- **Fibre** to allow the gut to push food along efficiently. Most fibre is plant material that we can't digest.

1 People who are starving are **undernourished**. As well as being underweight, the lack of food can cause a **reduced resistance to infection** – they are less able to fight off disease. Children fail to grow and develop normally, and women may have **irregular periods**.

2 People who don't eat a balanced diet are **malnourished**, and their health will suffer in some way. In the developed world, people are more likely to be overweight than underweight.

3 A lack of a particular vitamin or mineral will cause a **deficiency disease**; for example, a lack of vitamin D can cause rickets, a condition in which the bones don't develop properly.

● Balancing energy input and output

A key idea here is that of metabolic rate:

- **metabolism** is the general term for the chemical reactions inside your body;
- **metabolic rate** refers to the speed or rate of these reactions – it's basically the same as the rate of **respiration**, because respiration provides the energy that all the other reactions need.

People with a **high metabolic rate** will tend to be thin, and can eat a lot of food without putting on weight. People with a **low metabolic rate** tend to be overweight, and a higher proportion of their food will be stored as fat.

The amount of energy you need from food depends on:

- your **age** – young people tend to have a higher metabolic rate than older people;

■ If you want to stay healthy, five words of advice: eat plants, exercise, don't smoke

- your **sex** – boys tend to have a higher proportion of muscle-to-fat than girls do, and muscle has a higher metabolic rate – it's not sexist, it's biology;
- your **genes** – some people **inherit** a tendency to have a high or low metabolic rate, or a certain muscle-to-fat ratio.

And, of course, it depends on how much exercise you do. **Active muscles** have a very **high metabolic rate**. When we exercise, our metabolic rate **stays high** for quite a while after exercise, so you can see that exercise is a great way to control weight.

How much energy do we need?

- All of us need a certain amount of energy, which we get from our food.
- Proteins, carbohydrates and fats **all contain energy**.
- This energy is used for many different reactions in the body, including the movement of muscles and to keep warm.
- **Exercise** (moving muscles) increases the amount of energy expended by the body.

The only way to lose weight is to change the input/output balance, which means to reduce the energy content of your diet and be more active. The trick is to find the willpower to do it. Claims such as 'eat yourself slim' are unlikely to have any scientific basis.

check your understanding

12 Match the terms A–C to the spaces 1–3 in the paragraph below. *(3 marks)*

A glucose   B metabolic rate   C energy requirements

Of all sporting events, the Tour de France is one of the most demanding. Cyclists are on their bikes for long periods and for many days, so their ____1____ will be very high. It has been estimated that their daily energy needs are 30 000 kJ, while the average male of the same age needs about 12 500 kJ. The cyclists take regular drinks containing ____2____, our body's immediate source of energy. Being so active, these athletes will have a high ____3____.

13 Compared with most males of the same age, do cyclists usually have: *(1 mark)*
   A a high muscle-to-fat ratio and a low metabolic rate?
   B a low muscle-to-fat ratio and a low metabolic rate?
   C a high muscle-to-fat ratio and a high metabolic rate?
   B a low muscle-to-fat ratio and a high metabolic rate?

14 The labels on a chocolate bar state that it contains 1000 kJ. The table shows the energy expended by an average 25 year old female office worker. For how long would the individual need to be doing the following activities in order to work off the chocolate bar?
   a) Swimming.
   b) Sitting watching TV.   *(2 marks)*

Activity	Energy used in kJ/min
Standing, cooking	9
Sitting, watching TV	5
Walking briskly	15
Climbing stairs	28
Swimming	35
Dancing	19
Jogging	27

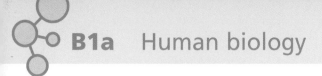

Problems with 'bad' diets

Problem – we like the foods that give us the most energy. Most of us like fatty foods, such as chicken tikka masala, pepperoni pizza, cheeseburgers and chocolate, because many of the flavour chemicals that we find so appealing are only found dissolved in fat.

● The problems of too much food

In the developed world, an increasing number of people are overweight or **obese**, which means grossly overweight.

Obesity can cause these health problems:

- **heart disease** (see below);
- **high blood pressure** – the heart has to work hard to pump blood around all that extra body tissue;
- extra strain on the joints, especially the knees, which may develop **arthritis**;
- **diabetes** – a common disease with a lot of complications.

● Too much salt is also a problem

Salt can cause high blood pressure or **hypertension** in about one in three people. It's easy to exceed the recommended daily dose of 6 g of salt.

● High cholesterol levels can lead to cardiovascular disease

Although cholesterol is a natural substance needed by cells, too much cholesterol in the blood leads to an increased risk of **coronary heart disease** and diseases of the **blood vessels**. The arteries become narrower due to a build-up of **fatty deposits** inside them. When vital arteries like the **coronary artery** get blocked, not enough oxygen reaches the heart muscle. Part of the heart muscle dies, and a **heart attack** results.

Cholesterol levels in the blood are affected by:

- the amount produced by the **liver**;
- the amount in the foods we eat – animal fats found in eggs, cream and fatty meat are especially high in cholesterol;
- heredity – some people have a high cholesterol level and watch what they eat.

What's the link between high cholesterol and heart disease?

- Cholesterol is a type of fat, so it doesn't dissolve in water. In order to be transported in the blood, has to be attached to protein molecules, called **lipoproteins**.

■ Most foods contain some salt to start with, *more* salt is added when food is processed, and many of us add *even more* salt at the table

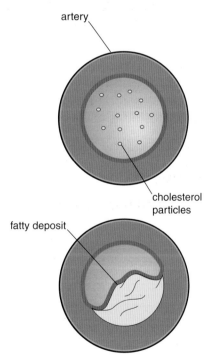

■ A healthy artery (top); the one below shows signs of coronary heart disease, the gap is narrower and blood flow will be reduced

- There are two types: **high-density (HDL)** and **low-density lipoprotein (LDL)**. LDLs are 'bad'. LDLs carry cholesterol from the liver and take it to other cells in the body. This is when it can lead to a build-up of deposits in arteries. HDLs are 'good'. They 'mop up' cholesterol and take it in the opposite direction, from body cells to the liver.
- It's all about balance. You want a high ratio of HDL to LDL in the blood.

Saturated and unsaturated fats

Saturated fats **raise** the cholesterol levels because they **increase** the amount of cholesterol the liver releases, and **reduce** the amount it takes in.

Unsaturated fats **lower** blood cholesterol by increasing its release from the body. They also improve the HDL–LDL balance.

All fats should be eaten in moderation, but the type of fat in the diet is also important. Saturated fats are common in **animal products** – meat, full-fat milk, cream and butter. Unsaturated fats are found in **fish oils** and **vegetable oils**. Processed food often contains a high proportion of saturated fat and/or salt.

Statins can lower cholesterol

Statins are relatively new drugs that can lower cholesterol levels. They work by blocking the enzyme that makes LDLs in the liver. They seem to be potentially life-saving drugs, but there could be side effects.

To find out, the British government carried out an **independent survey**, which means that they had no connection with the manufacturers. The sample was large – over 6000 patients were tested, so the results were **reliable**.

Studies like these need **two groups**: one group that has taken statins and another control group, as identical as possible, that has not taken statins.

They found that people who had taken statins had significantly lower cholesterol levels than the control group.

check your understanding

⑮ The term 'risk factor' means that you are more likely to suffer from a particular disease.

List two risk factors for heart disease.   (2 marks)

check your understanding

⑯ Match up the terms A–E with gaps 1–5 in the paragraph.   (5 marks)

A statins   B obese   C side effects
D saturated fat   E heart disease

My aunt says that my uncle is a walking heart attack. He's 6 feet tall but weighs 22 stone, so he's ___1___. Also, he's a long-distance lorry driver and he eats in motorway services and transport cafés. He smokes, and his favourite food is steak, egg and chips. His diet is high in ___2___. He complains of chest pains, and the doctor said that he has the symptoms of ___3___. They did a blood test and his cholesterol level was high. The prescribed him some ___4___ but he is worried about taking them as there could be ___5___.

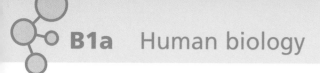

Fighting disease

There are two types of disease.

1 **Infectious** – diseases that you can catch. These are caused by **pathogens**, which are **disease-causing microorganisms**. The main microorganisms are **bacteria** and **viruses**.
2 **Non-infectious** – diseases you can't catch. These are caused by other factors, such as **lifestyle** (diet, smoking, etc.), your **genes**, or simply **getting older**.

Diseases caused by bacteria	Diseases caused by viruses
Food poisoning	HIV/AIDS
Cholera	Influenza
Typhoid	Colds
Leprosy	Chicken pox

● Bacteria are very small, but a major cause of disease

- Bacteria are tiny, single-celled organisms. Up to 1000 or more bacteria can fit inside one of your cells.
- Only a few types of bacteria cause disease. Most are harmless and many are useful.
- Bacteria cause disease when they multiply inside our bodies.

● Viruses make bacteria look big

- Viruses are so small that, even with the best light microscope, you can't see them – you need an electron microscope.
- Viruses cannot reproduce on their own. They reproduce by getting inside your cells and using their own DNA to instruct the cell to make more viruses. The new viruses burst out of the cell and go on to infect more cells.

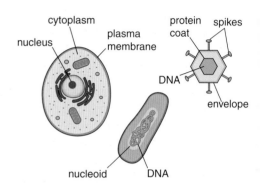

■ Simple diagrams of a human cell (left), a bacterial cell (centre) and a virus (right) (not to scale)

The **symptoms** of disease are caused in two ways. Bacteria and viruses produce **toxins** that interfere with the normal functioning of the body. Viruses **damage our cells** when they burst out. Painkillers like paracetamol will only make you feel better, but won't get rid of the bacteria or virus.

● What happens when microbes get inside the body?

This is where the **immune system** is needed. We have a number of different types of **white blood cells** whose job is to **recognise** these 'foreign' pathogens.

1 Once a pathogen has been identified, some white blood cells will make **antibodies** that attach to the pathogen so that it can be destroyed.
2 The body can make thousands of different antibodies, tailor-made for particular pathogens. So if the chicken pox virus gets into our blood, we can respond by making anti-chicken pox antibodies.

3 Some white blood cells produce **antitoxins**, which counteract the toxins (poisons) released by pathogens.

4 Some white blood cells **ingest** (engulf) pathogens or take them into the cell, where they are destroyed.

● Vaccines prepare the immune system

If the body meets a disease for the first time, it will have no antibodies for that disease. **Vaccination or immunisation** is used to protect against particular deadly diseases **before** infection.

A **vaccine** contains something that will **stimulate** the immune system to make the right antibodies without causing the disease. Vaccines can be made with **dead pathogens**; live but **weakened** (harmless) **pathogens**; or **purified antibodies**. If the pathogen gets into the body of a vaccinated person, that person will be **immune** to the pathogen. The more people who are vaccinated against a particular disease, the less likely the disease is to spread.

Vaccines have saved millions of lives. However, some vaccines may have serious **side effects**. Recently a study claimed a link between the measles, mumps and rubella (**MMR**) vaccine and **autism** in children. Some parents opted not to give the vaccine to their children. The controversy has since died down because there is very little evidence to support the claim.

It's all about weighing up the **risks**. Ask yourself:

● What are the chances of getting the disease?
● What are the chances of being damaged by the vaccine?

With measles the chances of getting complications like pneumonia are about one in 15, and about one in 500 die from the disease. The chance of having a problem with the vaccine is about one in 1 million.

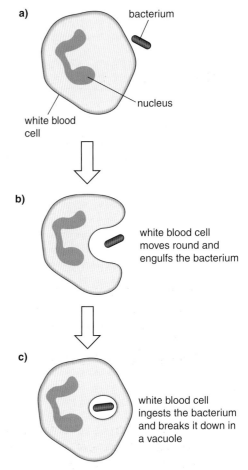

■ A white blood cell engulfing and destroying a bacterium – enzymes are discharged in the vacuole of the white blood cell, and break down the bacterium

check your understanding

⑰ State the three ways in which white blood cells defend against pathogens. *(3 marks)*

⑱ It is recommended that all children are vaccinated against measles because:

A measles can cause autism.
B vaccination protects against other infectious diseases.
C measles is a serious disease that can result in death.
D there is a risk that they will catch the antibodies for the disease from other children. *(1 mark)*

The fight against disease – then and now

Two hundred years ago, the treatment of infectious diseases left a lot to be desired. People had never heard of bacteria and viruses, and the need to be clean and avoid infection was not appreciated. You went into hospital at your peril.

Semmelweiss: a hero in the war against disease

In 1840, in Vienna Hospital, **Ignaz Semmelweiss** noticed that a lot of pregnant women (about 12%) were getting infections and dying soon after childbirth. He noticed that doctors would examine the women straight after treating other patients, or even after examining dead bodies. The need to wash their hands was not appreciated. Semmelweiss said that cadaveric material ('goo' from dead bodies) was being transferred and was causing the disease.

Semmelweiss told the doctors on his ward to **wash their hands** in **antiseptic**, and within a short time the death rate fell to 2%.

The antiseptic was killing bacteria, although the doctors and scientists didn't know that. The link between bacteria and disease wasn't established for another 20 years.

Antibiotics and 'superbugs'

Antibiotics are medicines that kill bacteria inside the body. They can't kill viruses. Before antibiotics were discovered, infectious diseases could not be treated, so the mortality rate was very high.

Due to **over-use** of antibiotics, some strains of bacteria are now resistant to one or more antibiotics. **MRSA** stands for methicillin-resistant *Staphylococcus aureus*. The antibiotic methicillin is no longer effective against that particular strain of the bacteria *Staphylococcus aureus*. The media gave the name **superbugs** to **antibiotic-resistant bacteria**.

This could be very bad news. There are more and more strains of bacteria getting resistant to more and more antibiotics. If no antibiotics were effective, we would be back to the days before penicillin – no treatment and a high death rate.

The good news is that we are developing new antibiotics all the time. Doctors also do not use antibiotics to treat minor infections. This **slows down** the rate of development of new strains of resistant bacteria.

The story of antibiotic resistance is a good illustration of how evolution works

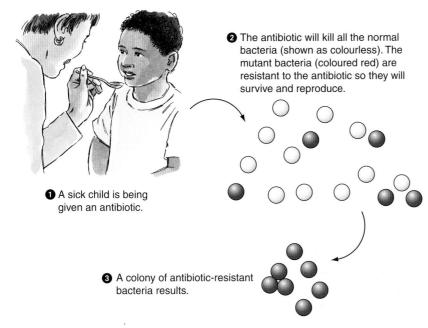

❶ A sick child is being given an antibiotic.

❷ The antibiotic will kill all the normal bacteria (shown as colourless). The mutant bacteria (coloured red) are resistant to the antibiotic so they will survive and reproduce.

❸ A colony of antibiotic-resistant bacteria results.

■ Development of a strain of bacteria resistant to an antibiotic

Three steps to antibiotic resistance:

1 Bacteria exist in vast numbers, and there is variation in the population.
2 Some bacteria are naturally resistant to penicillin. This could be due to a chance **mutation**, or it may be due to a gene that the bacteria have had for a long time.
3 The resistant bacteria **survived** and **reproduced**, passing their resistance genes on to the next generation. This is **natural selection**. The population of resistant **bacteria** increased.

Mutations and the chance of epidemics

Mutations occur in both bacteria and viruses. In viruses, a new mutation could make the current vaccine ineffective. This happens every year with different strains of the flu virus – a **new vaccine** has to be developed to fight the new virus strain.

If a new vaccine is not developed quickly, the disease will spread rapidly because people are not immune to it. A widespread outbreak is called an **epidemic**. An epidemic that spreads across continents is called a **pandemic**.

check your understanding

⑲ Explain why it is important to avoid over-use of antibiotics.　*(2 marks)*

⑳ Use the information in this section to relate the contribution of Semmelweiss in controlling infection to how we might solve modern problems with the spread of infection in hospitals.　*(2 marks)*

㉑ 'Avian flu' is a virus that can be spread from one bird species to another bird species. At present there are very few cases of the virus spreading from birds to humans. Avian flu could become a pandemic if:　*(1 mark)*

A the virus becomes resistant to antibiotics.
B the virus mutates so that a new strain can infect humans.
C birds are no longer immune.
D not enough birds are vaccinated.

Adapt and survive

Where a species is found (its **distribution**) depends on various environmental factors, such as:

- amount of light (if it is a plant);
- temperature;
- availability of water;
- availability of oxygen and carbon dioxide.

■ The walrus is a large animal with a thick layer of blubber, so that it can swim in the coldest arctic waters without losing too much heat

● Polar animals are adapted to reduce heat loss

- Many polar animals have a compact, rounded shape to keep their **surface area** as **small as possible**. This minimises heat loss.
- They also have a thick layer of **blubber** – tissue rich in fat that **insulates** them from the cold. This fat can also act a **food reserve**.
- Thick fur traps a layer of insulating air.
- Animals such as the polar bear and arctic fox have white fur so that they are **camouflaged** – making it easier for them to hunt in snow.

● Desert plants are adapted to reduce water loss

Most plants need a regular supply of water, but the cactus can survive in the desert by **absorbing** as much water as it can when available, and **losing as little as possible**.

- The leaves of most plants have a large surface area to trap light, but they also lose a lot of water. In the cactus the leaves have been reduced to spines. This **reduces surface area** for water loss and provides useful protection.
- They have a **thick, fleshy stem** that can **store water**, and a **thick waxy outer layer** so that very little water is lost by evaporation.
- Some cacti have shallow but **extensive roots** to absorb water when it rains. Others have **deep roots** to reach underground water.

■ Survival in the desert is all about minimising water loss

● Desert animals are adapted to increase heat loss

Animals that live in hot, dry conditions have a problem. The best way to lose heat is by evaporation, and that means sweating, but desert animals can't afford to lose all that precious water.

- Camels have **very little fat** under their skin, where it would insulate them and prevent them from losing heat. Instead, they

■ The body shapes of desert animals are adapted to have a large surface area-to-volume ratio, which increases heat loss

have all their fat in a hump (or two) on their back. When food is scarce they can live off this fat.
- They have thin (or no) hair, making heat loss easier.
- They have a long neck and legs, giving a **large surface area-to-volume ratio**, which increases heat loss.

Avoiding predators is vital

There are many different ways to avoid being eaten.

- Some plants and animals have **weapons** and **armour**. Plants such as roses, cacti and hawthorn have spines or **thorns**, and animals such as hedgehogs and porcupines have **spines**.
- Some are **camouflaged** so that predators don't notice them. Stick insects look like the plants they feed on, and are very slow so that predators don't notice their movement.
- Some animals produce **toxins** (poisons), and often use **warning colours** to advertise the fact. Wasps and poison arrow frogs are good examples.

check your understanding

❶ State two ways in which a prey animal may be adapted to deter predators. *(2 marks)*

❷ A fieldwork survey measured the distribution of moss growing in different parts of the school grounds. More moss was found on grass underneath a tree compared with the grass on the football field.

Which of the following is the most likely explanation?
(1 mark)

A Moss needs bright light.
B Moss is pale green so it was more camouflaged on the football field and wasn't seen.
C There is more water available under the tree.
D There are more soil nutrients on the football pitch.

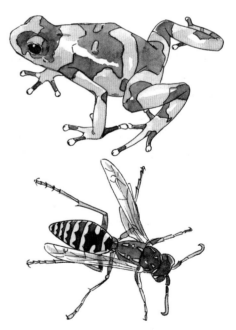

■ 'Go away, I'm poisonous' – a poison arrow frog and a wasp

Populations and competition

A **population** is a group of individuals of the same species that live in a particular environment – their **habitat**.

The **size** of the population is always **limited** by a combination of three factors: **competition, predation** and **disease**.

● The effect of competition

Usually, reproduction results in many more individuals being created than can possibly survive. The **resources** needed for survival will, sooner or later, be in **short supply**.

An animal might compete with members of its own species, or with other species, for:

- food;
- mates;
- territory.

And a plant might compete with other plants for:

- light;
- water;
- soil minerals.

■ Something's got to give – they can't go on reproducing forever

● Effects of predation and disease

Predators, such as foxes, eat **prey**, such as rabbits. The numbers of predators and prey are dependent on each other. For instance, if there is a large population of rabbits in an area, there will be more food for the foxes, who will be able to raise more cubs. The increase in the number of foxes will result in a reduction in the rabbit population – so there is a pattern of rising and falling numbers.

Infectious diseases, caused by **pathogens** such as bacteria, viruses and fungi, can seriously reduce or even wipe out a population. Often, if a population is too **overcrowded**, disease will spread more rapidly. In these circumstances, only those lucky individuals whose **immune system** is good enough will survive.

● Competition between species

Different species can also compete for the same resources. Red squirrels are native to the UK. Grey squirrels were introduced from the USA, and in almost all areas the population of greys has increased while the population of reds has declined. This may have been due to competition for food.

Prey animals compete with each other for food, and to avoid being eaten.

To **avoid competition**, different plants growing in the same habitat may produce flowers at **different times** so they don't compete for pollinating insects.

● Effects of humans

- Humans are predators of some species, such as fish.
- They may also compete with some species for food e.g. fishermen and seals.
- They may cause **pollution** that affects the supply of food for a species.
- They may **destroy habitats** by building, or **trample** plants and kill them.

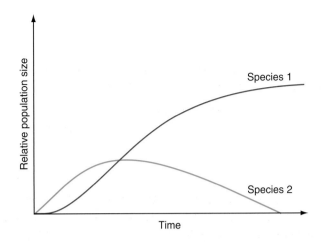

■ The populations of two plant species over time can be explained if one plant has grown so large that its leaves block light for the other plant, and its roots reach most of the available water. Species 1 out-competes species 2

check your understanding

❸ The graph shows numbers of nesting pairs of peregrine falcons in the USA.
   a) Peregrine falcons have no predators. Suggest **one** reason for the decline in numbers up to 1980. *(1 mark)*
   b) Suggest **two** reasons for the recovery in the population. *(2 marks)*

❹ Bats have an adaptation called echolocation that enables them to detect and measure the distance to objects by emitting a high-pitched sound. Bats eat the same prey – insects – as other birds. Which of the following is **not** an advantage given by the echolocation adaptation? *(1 mark)*

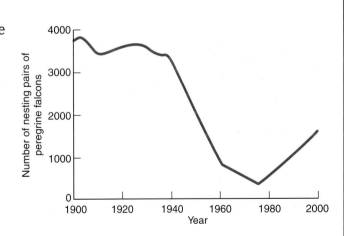

   A Bats can use the high-pitched sound to attract mates.
   B Bats can hunt at night, so competition with other predator species is reduced.
   C At night there could be fewer other species that may prey on the bats.
   D At night more insects come out as there are fewer predators.

Variation and inheritance

It's obvious that all people are different – even identical twins will have their differences. **Variation** is to be found in all other species too.

How do organisms vary?

■ Dogs and sheep look very different from each other because they're from different species – but despite what you might think, the sheep all vary too

Consider your year group at school. You can see variation in countless different ways: height, weight, eye colour, shoe size, blood group and intelligence, to name but a few.

There are two causes of variation

1 Your **genes**:
- all living things have **characteristics** that are **similar** to their **parents**;
- this is because an organism's characteristics are **controlled by genes**;
- genes are **instructions** that control the way an **organism grows and develops**;
- we inherit a **random mixture** of genes from **both parents**, which is why we are different, even from our brothers and sisters.

2 Your **environment**:
- the conditions in which you have lived and grown up;
- the food you have eaten, the experiences you have had and the pathogens you have been exposed to.

Putting the two together, are you the way you are because of your genes, or is it your environment? It's a complicated mixture of both. People often call this the **nature versus nurture** argument.

Some characteristics are determined by **genes only**. Examples include eye and hair colour (yes, you can dye your hair, but that's cheating), blood group and inherited diseases such as cystic fibrosis.

Other factors, such as height, are controlled by both – you will inherit the genes to grow to a certain height, but you will not do so without a good diet.

● Genes, chromosomes and DNA

When you first looked down a microscope at some cells, perhaps from your cheek, you will have seen the **nucleus** as just a dot.

But what really goes on in the nucleus is the key to life itself.

1 The nucleus contains a lot of DNA. Usually, it's all spread out so you can't see any detail.

2 If a cell is going to divide, it will roll its DNA up into X-shaped structures called **chromosomes**.

3 Most human cells have 23 **pairs of chromosomes**. There are two number ones, two number twos, etc. We can't draw them all here.

4 A chromosome is one long, tightly coiled DNA molecule. The **genes** are regions of DNA, like words on a long piece of tape. There are hundreds or even thousands of genes in a single chromosome.

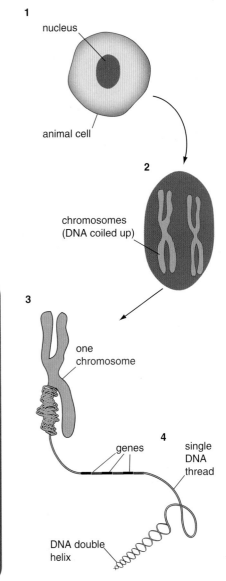

check your understanding

❺ Identical twins have exactly the same genes, so you would expect that any differences would be due to their environment.
   a) Suggest a reason why studies on identical twins show less variation in characteristics controlled by the environment compared with the variation observed in other schoolchildren. *(2 marks)*
   b) Suggest a possible reason why studies of identical twins who were raised apart are often seen to be invalid. *(1 mark)*

❻ Which of these statements is **not** true? *(1 mark)*

   A Genes are made from DNA.
   B Different forms of genes are called chromosomes.
   C Human cells contain 23 pairs of chromosomes.
   D Most human cells contain a complete set of genes.

Reproduction and cloning

Asexual reproduction produces clones

- **Asexual** means non-sexual.
- Asexual reproduction involves just **one parent**.
- There is no mixing of genetic information, so all cells made are genetically identical to the parent – they are **clones**.
- In asexual reproduction, a whole new organism is made.
- Many different species reproduce asexually – bacteria, yeasts, many plants and some animals (such as greenfly).

■ Asexual reproduction in a strawberry plant

Sexual reproduction gives variety

- **Sexual** reproduction involves **two parents**.
- There is a **mixing** of **genetic information** so that each new individual is **unique**.
- In sexual reproduction, the mother and father produce **sex cells**, or **gametes**.
- The male gametes are **sperm**, the female gametes are **eggs** (**ova**).

Cloning

Identical twins result from **one fertilised egg splitting into two**, each of which develops into a baby. This is natural cloning.

Cloning plants is relatively easy.

1 **Taking cuttings**
   Gardeners or farmers can simply take a cutting from a plant they want to clone, put it into the right conditions, and it will grow into a copy of the parent plant.

2 **Tissue culture**
   A small piece of plant tissue – perhaps just a few cells – is put into a growth medium. The cells multiply, and are then separated. Each cell in its own growth medium multiplies into a clump of cells that grows into a new plant.

Whole animals can be cloned in two ways. Farm animals, such as sheep and cattle, do not reproduce asexually, but there are ways to produce identical copies of individual animals.

Can we clone humans?

1 Can we? – the **science** question
2 Should we? – the **ethics** question.

The answer to question 1 is not yet – the process is just the same as cloning a sheep but no human has been cloned yet because the process is not reliable. The answer to question 2 depends on an individual's opinions, which may be influenced by **religious** or **ethical** beliefs.

a) Taking cuttings

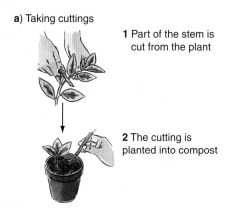

1 Part of the stem is cut from the plant

2 The cutting is planted into compost

b) Tissue culture

cell growth to form a cluster of cells

sterile tube

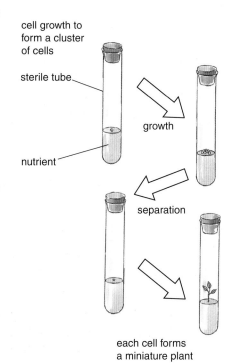

growth

separation

nutrient

each cell forms a miniature plant

1 Embryo transfer

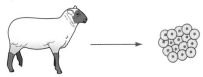

1. An embryo (clump of developing cells) is removed from a pregnant animal.

2. The embryo is split into a number of smaller clumps of cells.

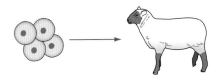

3. Each new embryo is inserted into the uterus of another host mother.

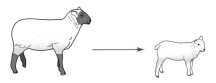

4. Some of the host mothers become pregnant and give birth to offspring.

2 Adult cell cloning

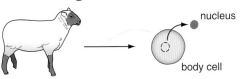

1. Take a cell (e.g. from the skin) from the animal to be cloned, and remove its **nucleus**. Remember that a **full set of genes** is present in the nucleus of **every cell**.

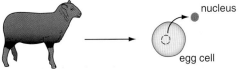

2. Take an **unfertilised egg** from the same species and remove its **nucleus**.

3. Put the nucleus from the animal to be cloned into the unfertilised egg.

4. The **fused** egg is stimulated with a **mild electric shock** so that it starts to develop into an **embryo**.

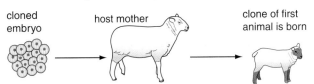

5. Implant the embryo into a uterus. The embryo is a clone of the adult from which the single cell was taken.

There are several ways of cloning human tissue for treatment. **Tissue culture** could be used to grow cloned replacement tissue, for example skin for burns patients. Tissue could also be grown from an embryo cell that had its nucleus replaced with one from the patient. However, cloning cells from embryos kills the embryo. Alternative methods are being researched, such as **fusion cell cloning**. A single adult cell (for example, from skin) is **fused** with cytoplasm from an egg cell. The fused cell (a clone of the original adult cell) can divide into many different types of cell.

check your understanding

7 Describe the difference between adult cell-cloning and embryo transfer techniques. *(2 marks)*

8 When a gardener takes a cutting, each cutting grows into a new plant that looks identical to the original plant. The best explanation for this is that: *(1 mark)*

    A the gardener used identical compost to grow the cuttings.
    B the plants have identical gametes.
    C the plants have identical genes.
    D the gardener used pollen from a plant of an identical species to fertilise the cutting.

Genetic engineering

Using **genetic engineering**, scientists can add, remove or alter an organism's genes. There are exciting possibilities (e.g. genetically engineered bacteria can make insulin for diabetes) – but there might be problems too.

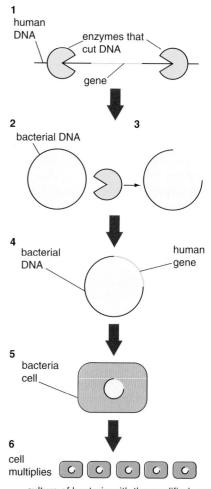

● Genetic engineering can change a characteristic by transferring a gene

Remember that different genes control the development of different characteristics.

The process of genetic engineering is as follows:

1 Find a gene for a useful characteristic in one organism.
2 **Cut it out** of the chromosome using an **enzyme**.
3 Cut open the DNA of the target organism.
4 Insert the cut-out gene into the organism's DNA.
5 Put the new **modified** DNA back into a cell.
6 As the cell grows and multiplies, all the new cells have copies of the modified DNA, and so have the desired characteristic.

● Genetic engineering can produce new varieties of crops

Genes from one plant can be transferred into another species of plant. This can produce a new variety with **increased yield**, or **better nutritional value**.

Genes from bacteria can also be transferred into plants. For example, a certain bacterium produces a substance which kills insects that destroy crop plants. Scientists cut out the **insecticide gene** and transfer it into crop plants such as maize and cotton. The **genetically modified** (GM) crops now produce their own insecticide, and resist insect attack.

● Genetic engineering can modify animals and plants as they develop

Genes can also be transferred to animal **embryos**. A solution containing genes that carry desired characteristics (such as disease resistance) is **injected** into the embryo cells. The embryo develops with the desired characteristic.

In plants, tiny metal particles coated with genes can be fired into plant cells. The full plants grown from these plant cells have the new characteristic.

● There are plenty of benefits for food production

As well as GM crops with better yield, nutrition or insect resistance, we could produce:

- crops that are **resistant** to **disease** or **herbicides**;
- salt-tolerant crops which can grow in salty areas that can't be farmed at the moment;
- crops that grow more quickly (by putting the growth genes from fast-growing species into slower-growing species);
- sheep that grow up to make useful products in their milk.

● But there are also problems

- Some people are concerned about the effect of eating GM crops on **human health**.
- Some people are worried that transplanted genes will **spread** into **wild plant populations** by cross-pollination. For example, there is a risk that common plants could become 'superweeds'.
- If other (harmless) insects feed on a GM crop that kills insect pests, biodiversity could be reduced.
- If farmers know they can spray weedkiller over a whole field and not harm the crop, will they kill all the other plants, including wild flowers?

If you are provided with unfamiliar information to evaluate, use this technique:

- What are the pros and cons given?
- Use the information provided, but check for people who might be biased or have unscientific opinions
- Use the evidence from data in graphs or tables to support your argument
- If there is no scientific evidence, there can be no conclusion – perhaps it is too early to tell.

check your understanding

9 Give an advantage to farmers of growing herbicide-resistant crops. *(1 mark)*

10 A variety of soya bean has been genetically modified to be resistant to herbicides. Some people are worried that GM crops may lead to a reduction in biodiversity. The explanation for this is: *(1 mark)*

A People will only want to eat the new crops, so old crop varieties will die out.
B Pollen from the herbicide-resistant crop could transfer to other plants.
C The whole field can be sprayed with weedkiller, so wild flowers will die.
D The farmer will use more pesticide, and so kill harmless insects.

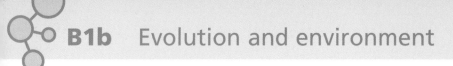

The fossil record

Evolution is one of the big ideas in biology. There are some important questions to be answered:

- How did life arise?
- Where do new species come from?
- Why are some species extinct?

We're not sure how life began – nobody was there

It's important to appreciate that the Earth is **extremely old**. Our current best estimate is that our planet is **4.6 billion years** old. That's 4 600 000 000 years. Scientists think life on Earth began 3.5 billion years ago.

- There are many different theories about how life began. Some are based on religion, others are more firmly rooted in science.
- There is a theory that the **first organic molecules** came to Earth on a **comet**, and then evolved into the complex organic molecules, such as proteins and DNA, that are needed for life.
- Another theory is that these preconditions for life developed on the Earth.

The first living things were like bacteria, tiny and **soft-bodied**, so they left very little **evidence** behind. As organisms evolved bigger and more complex bodies, more started to become **fossilised**.

Fossils have helped us piece it all together

Fossils are evidence that a species once existed. It could be a skeleton or shell, a leaf, a footprint or even a pile of dung.

Different layers of rock have different fossils, so we can often figure out what lived with what, and work out a **timeline**. We know that there were fish before amphibians, for instance.

So where did all the dinosaurs go?

There are many different species alive today, but they are far outnumbered by those that are **now extinct**. There are fossils of dinosaurs, but no living dinosaurs. How does extinction happen? A species may become extinct if:

- a **predator** or **disease** kills them;
- the climate or environment **changes too quickly** (humans are often the cause);
- a new species **outcompetes** them, usually for food.

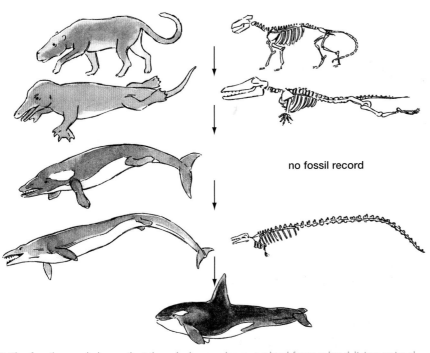

no fossil record

Very, very few organisms ever turn into fossils. Most were soft-bodied, many were eaten or just rotted away completely. Only a few died in just the right condition to become fossilised. Many species would have left **no trace** at all. The very earliest fossils have been **destroyed** by geological activity. Many fossils may still be **undiscovered**, or perhaps we have only **part of the skeleton**. This means that there are **gaps in the fossil record**.

But the fossil record shows that **organisms changed over time**. This is evidence for **evolution**.

■ The fossil record shows that the whale may have evolved from a land-living animal

● Tracing similarities and differences

Some species, such as humans and chimpanzees, have **similar characteristics**. Sometimes the fossil record suggests that an extinct organism may be the **common ancestor** of these similar species.

An **evolutionary tree** shows how these species could be related.

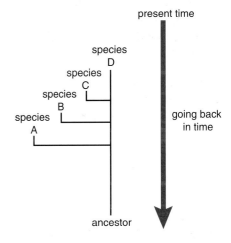

present time

species D

species C

species B

species A

ancestor

going back in time

check your understanding

⑪ The fossil record shows that some animals alive today have similar characteristics to animals that lived millions of years ago.

The word for this is: *(1 mark)*

A variation.
B competition.
C extinction.
D evolution.

How evolution happens

The trouble with evolution is that it is usually extremely slow. But there is strong evidence from fossils that it does happen, and that if you know where to look you can still see it happening today.

● Evolution starts with mutations

A **mutation** is a change in an organism's **DNA**.

There are three possible outcomes of a mutation:

1 It may be harmful, killing the organism.
2 It may have no effect at all.
3 Very occasionally it may be useful, for example giving new coloration, better eyesight or a stronger immune system. In this case the mutation will give the individual a **survival advantage**.

● Natural selection is the mechanism of evolution

The idea of evolution had been around for centuries, but it was **Charles Darwin** who first put forward a good idea about how it could happen. Darwin's theory was based on the following observations.

1 There are more organisms born **than can possibly survive**.
2 So there will be **competition** for food, mates, etc.
3 There is usually **variation** within a population due to individuals' genes (see page 24).
4 In the struggle to survive, some will be born with an advantage (see page 20). They will be **better adapted** to their environment.
5 There is more chance that a better-adapted individual will **survive** and **pass on their genes** to the next generation. The offspring that inherit these genes will have also an advantage, and so it goes on. This is **natural selection**.
6 Organisms that reproduce quickly, such as bacteria, will have more mutations in a given time. This means they can **adapt** to changing conditions more rapidly than a slow reproducing species.

● Evolution in action – rats and rat poison

You don't need to learn this example, but you need to be able to explain similar examples using scientific ideas. It's the same story as superbugs on page 18.

Rats have been a big problem for years. In the 1950s a new poison became available – Warfarin. This was very effective and killed many rats without harming other wildlife, humans or pets. But there are a lot of rats, and they breed very quickly. It wasn't long before Warfarin-resistant strains of rats appeared. How did that happen?

- When Warfarin was introduced, some populations already contained rats with a chance mutation that gave them resistance to the poison.
- Warfarin was a new environmental factor that killed normal rats.
- A few resistant rats survived, reproduced and passed on the resistance gene. They produced a new population of resistant rats.

Darwin's theories caused great controversy

Darwin came up with his idea for evolution in his twenties, but he knew that they would cause trouble, so he gathered evidence to support his theory for decades, and did not publish until he was about 50 years old.

- Darwin's theory went against common religious beliefs, which were based on the Bible. This said that God made all the plants and animals that live on Earth.
- There is now much evidence to support Darwin's theory. The fossil record grows more complete all the time.
- Darwin had no idea about DNA, genes or chromosomes, so he could not explain **how** characteristics were varied or passed on.

Other theories of evolution

Scientists may produce different **hypotheses** to explain similar observations. In 1809, the year Darwin was born, a Frenchman called Jean-Baptiste Lamarck put forward a theory for evolution. His idea was called the '**inheritance of acquired characteristics**'.

- Lamarck said that **useful changes** in a species were inherited, but these changes were **acquired** during the organism's lifetime.
- We now know that the environment can change characteristics (eating different food; going to the gym), but these changes can't be inherited.

■ Lamarck's explanation for the heron's long legs

check your understanding

⓬ Can you think of any evidence that disproves Lamarck's idea?　　　　*(1 mark)*

⓭ What is the key difference between Darwin's and Lamarck's theories?　　*(2 marks)*

How do humans affect the environment?

There are over 6 billion people on this planet. That's six thousand million. And the population of the world is expanding rapidly. Although the populations of richer countries, such as the UK, are relatively stable, in many countries the birth rate exceeds the death rate, and so the population is expanding.

● Effect on resources

1 A rising population needs more food, fuel and clean water.
2 Raw materials, including **non-renewable energy** resources, are rapidly being used up.
3 **Deforestation** is not just about using timber, but replacing rainforest with land used to grow crops to produce more food.
4 People want a higher **standard of living**, and more resources are used to make more cars, TVs or tumble dryers, or to travel to far-away places.
5 Expanding cities and more farms, landfill sites and quarries reduce the amount of land available for animals and plants.

● Production of waste

Extracting metals, quarrying rocks and drilling for oil produce waste. We dump vast quantities of household refuse and sewage into land, air and sea. When human activity dumps enough stuff to upset the natural balance of ecosystems, that's **pollution**.

Pollution can kill organisms (reduce local **biodiversity**), affect **habitats** for wildlife and change the **global environment**.

Air pollution:

● Carbon dioxide from **burning of fossil fuels** is thought to be causing **global warming** (see pages 36 and 54).
● **Smoke** and **soot** pollute the air we breathe.
● **Sulfur dioxide** from burning of fossil fuels can combine with water vapour in clouds to produce **acid rain**, which pollutes lakes and streams.

Land pollution:

● Pesticides and herbicides can affect populations of wild birds, insects and flowers.
● Other **toxic chemicals** from industrial waste, such as **heavy metals**, may be washed from land into water.

Water pollution:

● **Sewage** from farmland and water-treatment works can over-fertilise lakes and waterways and reduce the oxygen available for aquatic creatures (bacteria take all the oxygen).
● **Toxic waste** from industry, even tiny amounts, can kill species.

■ Since about 1800, improvements in medicine and food production have meant that many more people survive, and so go on to breed

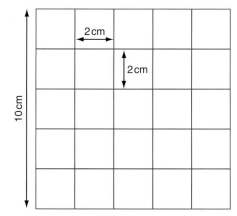

a 10 cm quadrat marked on a clear sheet

1. The quadrat is placed in a few randomly chosen places.
2. The number of lichens within the quadrat, or the area covered, is counted.
3. Only about 2% of the total site needs to be sampled to give an average.

■ Sampling means looking at a small part of the total data set

Indicators for air and water pollution

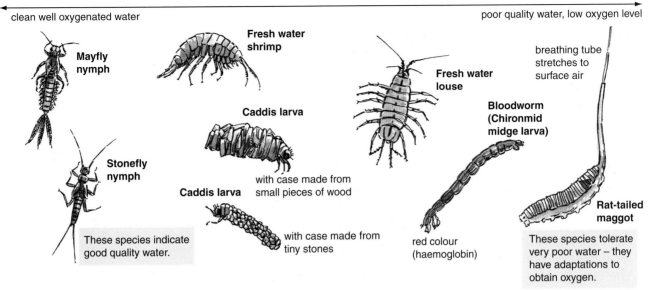

clean well oxygenated water ──────────────────────────► poor quality water, low oxygen level

Mayfly nymph

Fresh water shrimp

Fresh water louse

breathing tube stretches to surface air

Caddis larva

Bloodworm (Chironmid midge larva)

Stonefly nymph

Caddis larva

with case made from small pieces of wood

with case made from tiny stones

red colour (haemoglobin)

Rat-tailed maggot

These species indicate good quality water.

These species tolerate very poor water – they have adaptations to obtain oxygen.

■ Some organisms thrive when dissolved oxygen levels are low – their presence indicates polluted water

- The presence or absence of certain **aquatic invertebrates** can be used to indicate water quality.
- **Lichens** are very sensitive to pollutants so indicate clean air.

Sampling of indicator species requires a well planned investigation. When comparing two different locations:

- the more samples taken, the more **reliable** the estimate of population size will be;
- samples must be taken from **random locations** – this means the sample is likely to be **representative**, and you are not introducing **bias**;
- small variation is to be expected due to the random sampling, but an **anomalous** result may not be representative;
- a **consistently large difference** in the measurements at the same site by different groups could be due to a **systematic error** – for example, did the two groups use different-sized buckets to sample the water?

check your understanding

⑮ Match the words A–D with the spaces 1–4 in the text below.
(4 marks)

A deforestation   B acid rain   C global warming
D sewage

Burning wood releases sulfur dioxide, which causes
_____1_____ and carbon dioxide, which causes _____2_____.
The population is increasing, so uses more fuel and produces
more _____3_____ as well as causing _____4_____.

check your understanding

⑭ A fieldwork survey used quadrats to estimate the percentage cover of lichens growing on tree trunks in different areas of the school grounds.
a) Suggest two different areas to investigate, giving a hypothesis for why there might be a variation between the two areas. *(2 marks)*
b) Describe a method to determine where a sample should be taken *(1 mark)*
c) Explain why further samples should be taken. *(2 marks)*

Global warming

The Earth's etmosphere has been getting warmer in the past 200 years (**global warming**). Scientists think this is due to an increased **greenhouse effect**:

● What causes the greenhouse effect?

As in a greenhouse, the atmosphere is allowing **sunlight energy in**, but not letting all of it escape, so it gets hotter.

1 Temperatures on Earth result from a **balance** in **energy received** and **energy lost**.
2 The energy we get from the Sun is not changing, but we are **losing less**.
3 This is because we are **changing** the **composition** of our **atmosphere**. Gases such as **carbon dioxide** and **methane** act together to prevent heat from escaping.

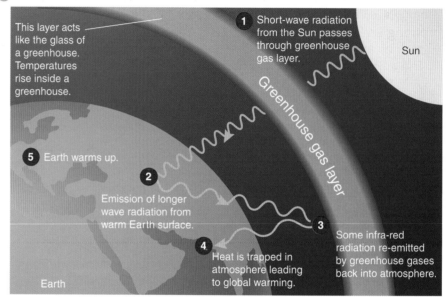

This layer acts like the glass of a greenhouse. Temperatures rise inside a greenhouse.

1 Short-wave radiation from the Sun passes through greenhouse gas layer.

Sun

Greenhouse gas layer

5 Earth warms up.

2 Emission of longer wave radiation from warm Earth surface.

3 Some infra-red radiation re-emitted by greenhouse gases back into atmosphere.

4 Heat is trapped in atmosphere leading to global warming.

Earth

Where does carbon dioxide come from?

Power stations, industry, cars and aircraft engines all **burn fossil fuels** to produce millions of tonnes of carbon dioxide every year. While there is a massive amount of **combustion** going on, **photosynthesis still absorbs carbon dioxide** from the atmosphere.

Cutting down forests (**deforestation**) is another problem. A lot of carbon is locked up in wood, so when we cut down and burn trees:

● more carbon dioxide is released;
● there are fewer trees to remove carbon dioxide from the atmosphere.

Methane gas (**CH_4**) is another greenhouse gas. Production of methane is increasing due to:

● cows belching and farting (**flatulence**) – cows release large amounts of methane, and as more cattle are being bred, more methane is produced;
● rice paddy fields producing methane – more rice is being grown as the world's population grows.

The effects of global warming are complex

The Earth's climate is a **complex system**. That means that its effect is impossible to predict exactly. However, some possibilities are:

- **Glaciers** and **ice caps** on Greenland and Antarctica will **melt** and drain into the sea, making **sea levels rise**.
- Higher temperatures make water **expand**, which scientists think may have more effect than melting ice on rising sea levels.
- Rising sea levels will flood low-lying areas with high populations such as large areas of the Netherlands.
- The extra fresh water may **disrupt ocean currents**. This could be a disaster for Britain – currently kept warmer by Atlantic currents.
- More **severe weather** – there could be more **hurricanes**.
- Higher temperatures could mean more evaporation, more clouds and a change in rainfall patterns.
- All over the world, ecosystems depend on the climate. Changes could disrupt plant growth and patterns of agriculture.

How can we be sure?

The evidence says that global warming is occurring, that ice caps are melting, and that all this is due to human activity.

- There is a **correlation** between increased greenhouse gases and global warming.
- A correlation may be a **coincidence**, but the rising temperature agrees with **climate prediction models** carried out by **different scientists** worldwide, making the conclusion more **plausible**.

The models also show that the effect of a rise of just a few degrees will be damaging. We may not feel the difference in our lifetime – but changes are clearly happening, so we must do something for future generations.

■ The Maldives are islands in the Indian Ocean. As much as 80% of the Maldives is less than 1 m above sea level. The most gloomy predictions say the Maldives could sink beneath the waves within the next few decades

check your understanding

⑯ List two factors contributing to increased methane concentrations in the atmosphere.   *(2 marks)*

⑰ Explain the effect of deforestation on carbon dioxide concentrations in the atmosphere. *(2 marks)*

⑱ The greenhouse effect is caused by: *(1 mark)*

   A a layer around the Earth that stops the Sun's radiation from reaching the Earth.
   B energy produced by nuclear power stations trapped by gases in the Earth's atmosphere.
   C energy radiated by the Sun trapped by gases in the Earth's atmosphere before it reaches the Earth's surface.
   D energy radiated by the Sun trapped by gases in the Earth's atmosphere after it is re-radiated from the Earth's surface.

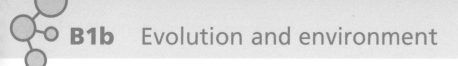

Sustainable development

At present, we are doing many things that are not **sustainable** – they can't go on for ever.

- Using fossil fuels, which are **non-renewable** and will eventually **run out**.
- Using up resources such as metal ores.
- Polluting ecosystems such as rainforests and coral reefs, which will not regenerate.

Sustainable development meets the needs of today's generation without damaging the planet for future generations.

● Sustainable development needs planning and co-operation

Planning is needed at global, regional and local levels. **Governments** need to **co-operate** and agree on **policies**. There has been some success in **international agreements**:

- many countries have agreed targets (the **Kyoto Agreement**) to reduce carbon dioxide emissions;
- many countries have signed up to **quotas** on **cod fishing**, which will **conserve** fish stocks.

Similar agreements could help **endangered species** that are used as food, fuel or medicines.

One problem is that we don't yet know which species lost due to **deforestation** e.g. in the Amazon may have been of future use, or what **undiscovered species** could have potential benefits. And does one country have **sole responsibility** for protecting the **biodiversity** of that country?

At a regional level:

- better **public transport** would reduce the number of car journeys;
- planning agreements for land use could prevent **loss of wildlife habitats**.

At a local level:

- there are more **recycling schemes** – recycling paper means that fewer forests are cut down; recycling glass and metals means that fewer quarries are dug;
- some schools and councils have made plans to use energy more **efficiently** – this **conserves** supplies of fossil fuels and **reduces pollution**;
- some homes and buildings use **renewable** energy resources – this also **conserves** supplies of fossil fuels and **reduces pollution**.

But it needs a collective will at every level to be successful.

check your understanding

⑲ Give two reasons why recycling should be part of a local council's sustainable development plan.

(2 marks)

⑳ National and international agreements on stopping the reduction in biodiversity are important because: *(1 mark)*

A it conserves supplies of fossil fuels.
B it reduces greenhouse gas emissions from rice paddy fields.
C it may be important for future development of new medicines.
D it means that fewer forests are cut down.

Atoms, elements and the Periodic Table

● All about atoms

- ● All substances are made of **atoms**.
- ● Atoms are extremely small – so small that it would take about 15 thousand million lined up against each other to make 1 cm.
- ● Atoms have a tiny central **nucleus**, around which there are **electrons**.
- ● Most of an atom is empty space – the electrons are a long way from the nucleus.

■ An atom: a nucleus surrounded by electrons

● All about elements

- ● A substance that is made of only one sort of atom is called an **element**.
- ● A gold bar in a bank vault contains just gold atoms, and nothing else.
- ● A **chemical symbol** represents one atom of an element, for example, O represents an atom of oxygen; Na represents an atom of sodium.
- ● Each element has a different symbol.
- ● When elements react, their atoms join with other atoms to form **compounds**. For example, hydrogen and oxygen react to form water.

exam tip

★ Learn this definition of an element – to get full marks you need to mention element in the definition

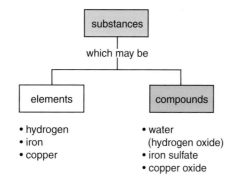

● All about the Periodic Table

- ● There are only about 100 different elements.
- ● These elements are shown in the **Periodic Table**.
- ● The **groups** contain elements with similar properties.
- ● The groups are the columns in the table, and are like families – different members look similar or behave like each other.

1 Alkali metals	2 Alkaline -earth metals											3	4	5	6	7 Halogens	0 Noble gases
																	He helium 2
Li lithium 3	Be beryllium 4											B boron 5	C carbon 6	N nitrogen 7	O oxygen 8	F fluorine 9	Ne neon 10
Na sodium 11	Mg magnesium 12				transition elements							Al aluminium 13	Si silicon 14	P phosphorus 15	S sulfur 16	Cl chlorine 17	Ar argon 18
K potassium 19	Ca calcium 20	Sc 21	Ti 22	V 23	Cr chromium 24	Mn manganese 25	Fe iron 26	Co cobalt 27	Ni nickel 28	Cu copper 29	Zn zinc 30	Ga 31	Ge 32	As 33	Se 34	Br bromine 35	Kr krypton 36
Rb 37	Sr 38	Y 39	Zr 40	Nb 41	Mo 42	Tc 43	Ru 44	Rh 45	Pd 46	Ag silver 47	Cd 48	In 49	Sn tin 50	Sb 51	Te 52	I iodine 53	Xe 54
Cs 55	Ba 56	La 57	Hf 72	Ta 73	W 74	Re 75	Os 76	Ir 77	Pt platinum 78	Au gold 79	Hg mercury 80	Tl 81	Pb lead 82	Bi 83	Po 84	At 85	Rn 86
Fr 87	Ra 88	Ac 89	Rf 104	Db 105	Sg 106	Bh 107	Hs 108	Mt 109									

Key

H ← symbol
hydrogen ← name
1 ← atomic number

■ The Periodic Table (elements 58–71 and 90–103 have been omitted)

So all you have to know are these four points:

1 Everything is made of **atoms**, which all have a **nucleus** surrounded by **electrons**.
2 When something is made of just one type of atom, then it is an **element** (like gold, for example) – each of the 100 elements (in the Universe) has been given a **chemical symbol**.
3 These elements combine to form **compounds**, such as the water we drink.
4 The elements are organised into the **Periodic Table**, where those of similar properties are found in the same **group** or column (look at Group 1).

check your understanding

❶ Draw and label a simple diagram of an atom.　　*(3 marks)*

❷ If some moon rock was found to be made of one sort of atom, would it be an element or a compound?　　*(1 mark)*

❸ Which sub-structure of the Periodic Table shows elements that have similar properties?　　*(1 mark)*

　A families　　B periods　　C groups　　D gatherings

❹ Which of these chemical symbols is NOT used in the Periodic Table?　　*(1 mark)*

　A Al　　B Cl　　C Fl　　D Tl

Reactions, formulae and balanced equations

● Compounds

- ● When elements react, their atoms join with other atoms to form **chemical bonds** in compounds.
- ● When atoms join up, their electrons can be given to, or taken from, another atom, but in most cases they are shared between the atoms.
- ● **Electron sharing** between atoms produces **molecules**.
- ● In a molecule of oxygen (O_2), there is only one type of atom, so this is an element.
- ● In a molecule of water (H_2O), there is more than one type of atom, so this is a compound.

water	carbon dioxide	ammonia	hydrogen chloride

■ Atoms join together to make compounds

● Formulae

We use atomic names and **chemical symbols** to show what is happening in chemical reactions – like this:

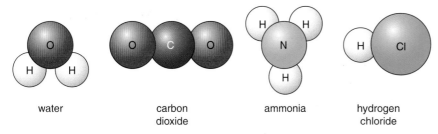

2Mg	+	O_2		2MgO
two magnesium atoms		one oxygen molecule		two magnesium oxide particles

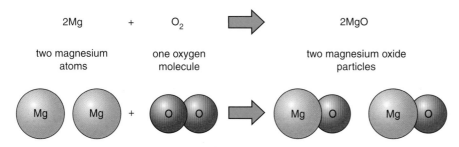

- ● The **formula** for oxygen is O_2 but its chemical symbol is O.
- ● The **formula** for magnesium oxide is MgO.

● Balanced equations

The **word equation** for this reaction is:

magnesium + oxygen → magnesium oxide

If we just write the formulae for the reactants and products:

$Mg + O_2 \rightarrow MgO$

then the equation is not **balanced**. Although there is one magnesium on each side, there are two oxygens on the left-hand side but only one oxygen on the right-hand side.

So MgO has to be doubled to give:

$Mg + O_2 \rightarrow 2MgO$

But now we have two Mg atoms on the right-hand side and only one on the other side. We correct this by putting 2Mg on the left:

$2Mg + O_2 \rightarrow 2MgO$

This is the **balanced chemical equation**.

So a balanced chemical equation has the same number of the same atoms on each side – they are just arranged differently.

● Never change the formula of a compound

- The formula of a compound shows the number and type of atoms that are joined together to make the compound.
- **No atoms are lost or made** during a chemical reaction – this is called **conservation of mass**.
- So the mass of the products equals the mass of the reactants and we write balanced equations showing the atoms involved.

Remember – the formula of magnesium oxide is MgO, showing that one atom of magnesium has joined with one atom of oxygen.

In the equation:

- 2MgO tells us two **formula** units of MgO are made;
- 2Mg tells us two **atoms** of magnesium are used;
- O_2 tells us one **molecule** of oxygen (two atoms joined) is used.

exam tip

★ Learn this equation, but make sure all the symbols are the right size, or else you will lose marks

---

check your understanding

5 Which parts of an atom are involved in chemical bonding? *(1 mark)*

   A the electrons   C neutrons in the nucleus
   B protons in the nucleus   D protons and neutrons in the nucleus

6 Write the word equation for the reaction between hydrogen and oxygen that produces water. *(2 marks)*

7 Write the balanced chemical equation for the reaction in question 6. *(2 marks)*

8 The following equations are not balanced. Write them out and balance them. *(2 marks each)*

$$CH_4 + O_2 \rightarrow CO_2 + H_2O$$

$$Na + H_2O \rightarrow H_2 + NaOH$$

$$H_2SO_4 + NaOH \rightarrow Na_2SO_4 + H_2O$$

Products from limestone

Limestone, containing the compound calcium carbonate ($CaCO_3$), is quarried and can be used as a building material.

How many uses? (six to remember):

1 **Building materials** – in buildings!
2 **Slaked lime** – to neutralise acidity.
3 **Mortar** – to stick bricks together.
4 **Cement** – to make mortar.
5 **Concrete** – for foundations of buildings.
6 **Glass** – in windows and drinking glasses.

■ A limestone quarry

● Making limestone useful

To do anything with limestone, other than use it as the rock, requires chemistry to modify its properties.

● **Building blocks** – quarried and cut to shape.
● **Cement** – heat limestone with clay.
● **Mortar** – mix cement with sand and water.
● **Concrete** – mix mortar with small stones (aggregate).
● **Glass** – heat a mixture of limestone, sand and sodium carbonate. This makes soda glass, one type of glass.

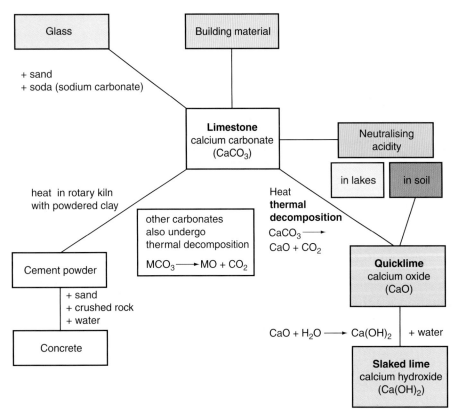

■ Uses of limestone

Modifying these materials

Different sorts of glass, such as coloured and toughened glass, are made by adding different chemicals to the molten glass mixture. Even a **smart material** such as photochromic glass, used to make sunglasses that react to sunlight, is made like this.

Concrete is very strong under compression, but quite weak if you try to bend it. **Reinforcing** it with steel rods produces a material that is strong under all types of strain.

The diagram opposite shows how heating calcium carbonate strongly will break it down into calcium oxide (quicklime) and carbon dioxide. Breaking down a compound using heat is called **thermal decomposition**.

It also shows the same reaction for other metal carbonates:

$MCO_3 \rightarrow MO + CO_2$

In this equation, M stands for a metal. All metal carbonates decompose on heating to form carbon dioxide and a metal oxide.

Advantages and disadvantages of using these products

Here are some factors to consider:

- Glass is easily broken.
- Glass does not scratch easily and is waterproof.
- Glass buildings let in lots of light, but can overheat in summer.
- Limestone buildings are good to look at.
- Limestone is fairly cheap and so are its products.
- Concrete can be poured into moulds to make different shapes.
- Limestone, concrete, and bricks and mortar are stronger than timber buildings.

check your understanding

9 Write the word equation *(2 marks)* and then the balanced chemical equation *(1 mark)* for the thermal decomposition of copper carbonate.

10 Write the word equation *(2 marks)* and then the balanced chemical equation *(2 marks)* for the reaction of water with quicklime (calcium oxide).

11 Which of the following reasons may be given for using limestone for building?   *(1 mark)*

   A It is difficult to carve.
   B Liquid limestone can be poured into moulds.
   C It polishes easily.
   D It can be modified by the addition of small amounts of other chemicals.

Extracting metals

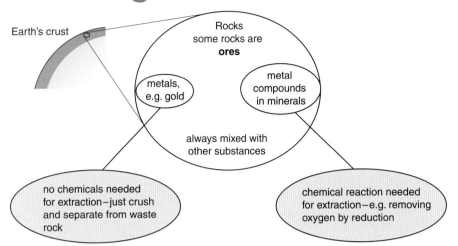

■ Extracting metals and metal compounds from the Earth's crust

The reactivity series

- Unreactive metals are found in the Earth as the metal itself.
- More reactive metals are found as minerals in **ores**. Minerals are compounds; a chemical reaction is needed to extract the metal.
- Metals that are **less reactive** than carbon can be extracted from their oxides by **reduction** with carbon.
- Iron oxide is reduced with **coke** in the blast furnace to make iron.
- Aluminium and titanium cannot be extracted from their oxides by reduction with carbon (they are **too reactive**).

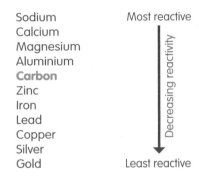

■ The reactivity series – note that aluminium is above carbon, but iron is below carbon

Purifying valuable metals using electrolysis

- **Copper** could be extracted by reducing with carbon, but the copper produced this way is impure. Copper has to be very pure to be a good conductor for use in electrical wiring.
- **Electrolysis** is used to extract copper from solutions containing copper compounds.
- But it uses large amounts of electricity, which is expensive in terms of fuel costs.
- **Aluminium** is also extracted by electrolysis.
- Electrolysis is expensive because much energy is needed to melt and pass electricity through the ore.
- Mining and concentrating the ore to start with is also expensive.
- However, metals such as copper and aluminium are so valuable that, even if the ore contains only a low percentage of metal, it is still economic to extract the metal.
- If the price of the metal goes down, it may not be economic to extract it from a **low-grade** ore.

Percentage of tin in ore	Price of tin per tonne	Income per tonne of tin produced	Mining cost per tonne of ore	Profit per tonne of tin produced
2.5	£5500	£138	£100	£38
1.5	£7000	£105	£100	£5
1.0	£6000	£60	£100	£40
1.0	£10 000	£100	£100	£0

You should be able to analyse data like these to explain how decisions about whether to mine metal ores depend on the concentration of metal and on the price

● Copper – the useful metal

- The supply of copper-rich ores is limited.
- Copper is so useful that, as we use up the metal-rich ores, we need to find new ways of extracting it from low-grade ores.
- Such methods include using bacteria, fungi and plants.
- These may be cheaper than current methods and, if used to extract copper from waste tips at old mines, would certainly be 'greener' than starting a new mine.

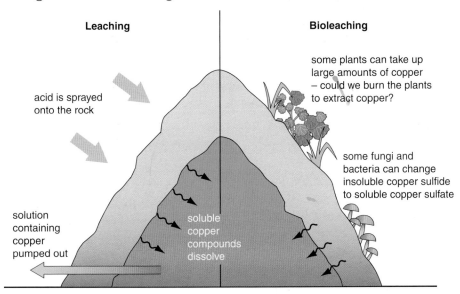

■ New methods of extracting copper from copper sulfide ores are slow, but use very little energy and do not cause sulfur dioxide emissions

check your understanding

⑫ Which metals are found as themselves in the Earth – the least reactive or most reactive? *(1 mark)*

⑬ By what process is iron extracted from its ore? *(1 mark)*

⑭ Which of the following metals cannot be extracted by reduction with carbon? *(1 mark)*

    A aluminium   C iron

    B copper   D lead

Quarrying, mining and recycling

● Quarrying

'Quarrying and mining have huge environmental impacts that can't be justified by the economic and social gains', said environmental protestor Aggy Clark.

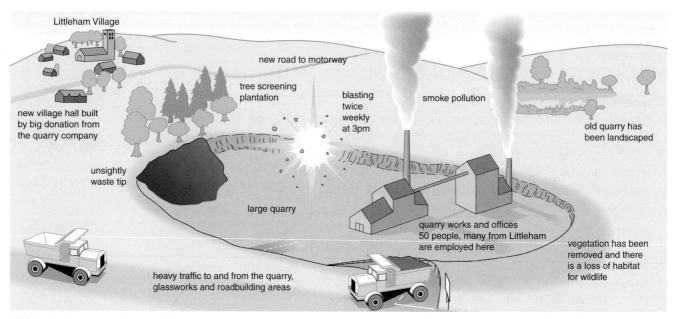

Littleham Village

new road to motorway

tree screening plantation

blasting twice weekly at 3pm

smoke pollution

old quarry has been landscaped

new village hall built by big donation from the quarry company

unsightly waste tip

large quarry

quarry works and offices 50 people, many from Littleham are employed here

vegetation has been removed and there is a loss of habitat for wildlife

heavy traffic to and from the quarry, glassworks and roadbuilding areas

■ A typical quarry and surrounding area

Look at the picture. Imagine what you would think of the quarry if you lived in the village.

Your **opinions** for or against quarrying may be:

- The quarry provides employment for your family and friends.
- The hole is ugly.
- The quarry provides necessary rock for producing building materials.
- There has been a loss of wildlife habitat.
- The lorries are dirty.
- The blasting is noisy.
- The works produce a lot of smoke pollution.

Do you have **evidence** to support all your opinions?

Taking public opinion into account, the quarry company might try to reduce the **environmental, economic and social impact** of the new quarry by:

- washing the lorries before they leave the site;
- blasting only twice a week;
- cleaning the smoke before it goes up the chimney;
- building new roads to link up with motorways;

- building a social centre/village hall;
- landscaping the site afterwards.

Mining and recycling

- Many of the issues about mining are exactly the same as those to do with quarrying.
- Mining also produces large amounts of waste rock when the ore is processed.
- We should **recycle** metals, because extracting them uses **limited resources** and is expensive in terms of **energy** and **effects on the environment**.
- Recycling also uses energy and costs money, but usually less than the cost of all the stages in mining and extracting metals from ores using chemical reactions.

Why recycle?

- **Price** – it's cheaper to recycle than to dig out more ore.
- **Limited resources** – it makes sense to conserve remaining ore.
- **Energy efficiency** – recycling uses 15% of the energy used in mining and metal extraction.
- **Landfill costs** – problems of rubbish disposal are avoided by recycling.
- **The environment** – no mining means fewer spoil heaps, and there are virtually no emissions of harmful gases (some methods of processing copper ore release sulfur dioxide).

Recycling difficulties

Separating mixed metals is very tricky – except for iron and steel, which are easily separated from other metals with a magnet.

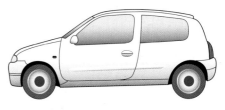

■ A car contains copper wiring and a radiator made from copper and brass – the total mass of copper is between 15 and 25 kg, and this can all be recycled

check your understanding

15 List three advantages of living close to a quarry. *(3 marks)*

16 List three disadvantages of living close to a quarry. *(3 marks)*

17 Which one of the following statements about why we should recycle metals is **not** true? *(1 mark)*

   A Recycling conserves finite supplies of metal ore.
   B Recycling conserves fossil fuel resources because less energy is used than in extracting metal from ores.
   C Recycling produces more carbon dioxide emissions than extracting metal from ores.
   D Recycling is more cost-effective than extracting metal from ores.

Using metals and alloys

Iron and steel

- Iron from the blast furnace (sometimes used as **cast iron**) contains about 96% iron.
- The impurities make it **brittle**, so cast iron has limited uses.
- Most iron is converted into **steels**.
- Steels are **alloys** – they are **mixtures** of iron, carbon and other metals.

Properties of alloys

Alloys are harder because the different-sized atoms distort the layers in the **structure**, making it more difficult for them to slide over each other.

Alloys can be designed to have properties for specific uses by varying the amounts of other metals that are added.

In the case of steel, it is the amount of carbon added that has the greatest effect on the properties:

- **low-carbon** steels are easily shaped;
- **high-carbon** steels are hard, but brittle;
- **stainless** steels resist corrosion.

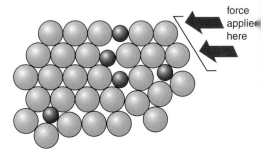

force applied here

■ Slip can't occur so easily in an alloy, because the structure has been distorted

The transition metals

- The **transition metals**, like other metals, are good conductors of heat and electricity, and can be bent or hammered into shape. They are useful as structural materials and for making things that must conduct heat or electricity.
- Copper is useful for electrical wiring and plumbing:
- it conducts electricity well;
- it is easily drawn into wires (**ductile**) or hammered into shapes (**malleable**).

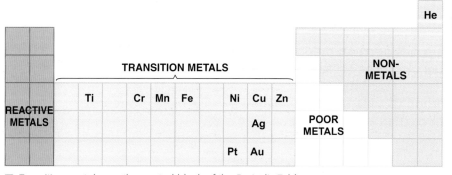

■ Transition metals are the central block of the Periodic Table

Aluminium and titanium

- **Low density** makes aluminium and titanium useful. The lightest bikes and the fastest jets are made from aluminium and titanium.
- Their **resistance to corrosion** is also useful. Aluminium window frames resist corrosion due to the tough oxide layer on them – so they don't need painting.

■ Aluminium and titanium are used to make aircraft because they resist corrosion and have low densities

Everyday metals

Many metals in everyday use are alloys. The pure metal would be too soft, so small amounts of similar metals are added to make them harder:

- stainless steel is used to make cutlery;
- coins are made of various alloys of copper and nickel;
- brass door handles are an alloy of copper and zinc;
- pure gold rings would be far too soft to keep their shape, so copper is added to increase their strength;
- aluminium is often alloyed with magnesium to make it strong enough for everyday use.

Smart alloys can return to their original shape after being deformed. Just like those super-twisty spectacle frames you've seen – they are made of a **shape-memory alloy**.

Benefits and drawbacks of using metals

Iron from the blast furnace is brittle, but strong under compression. It is good for manhole covers, but dangerous for building bridges and girders.

High-carbon steel is also brittle, so it is not suitable for use as steel girders, but it is good for drill bits – they need to be hard and stay sharp; low-carbon steel would be too soft.

Copper and aluminium are soft, so their harder alloys are used, rather than the pure metals – you can't make an aircraft of pure aluminium.

exam tip

★ In the exam, you may have to **evaluate** the benefits, drawbacks and risks of using different metals. You need to consider the metals' properties.

check your understanding

⑱ Give a reason why iron from the blast furnace is not very useful. *(2 marks)*

⑲ What is the really useful property of shape-memory alloys? *(1 mark)*

⑳ Which of the following is the main advantage of making coins from an alloy of copper instead of just copper? *(1 mark)*

    A The alloy is shinier.   C The alloy is harder.
    B The alloy is cheaper.   D The alloy is resistant to corrosion.

㉑ What is the most useful property of aluminium for making window frames? *(1 mark)*

    A It is lightweight.   C It is decorative.
    B It is reactive.   D It is soft.

Crude oil and fuels

- Crude oil is a **mixture** of a very large number of compounds, mainly **hydrocarbons**.
- **Hydrocarbons** are molecules made up of hydrogen and carbon atoms **only**.

A **mixture** consists of two or more elements or compounds **not chemically combined** together. The chemical properties of each substance in the mixture are unchanged.

Alkanes

- Most of the compounds in crude oil are **saturated hydrocarbons** called **alkanes**, which have the general formula C_nH_{2n+2}
- **Saturated** means you can't fit any more hydrogens into the molecule because there are no **carbon–carbon double bonds**.

Alkane molecules can be represented in the forms shown in the diagrams on the right.

Can you see that no more hydrogens will fit into the alkanes?

Fractional distillation

It is possible to **separate** the substances in a mixture by physical methods, including **distillation**. In **fractional distillation**, many liquids of different **boiling points** can be separated into **fractions**.

- Hydrocarbons in crude oil are separated by fractional distillation.
- Each fraction contains molecules with a similar number of carbon atoms (see table opposite).
- They are separated by heating and evaporating the hydrocarbons and allowing them to **condense** at different temperatures.
- The different fractions are easily separated because of their different boiling points.

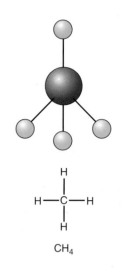

CH_4

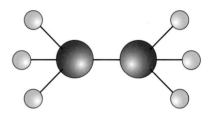

C_2H_6

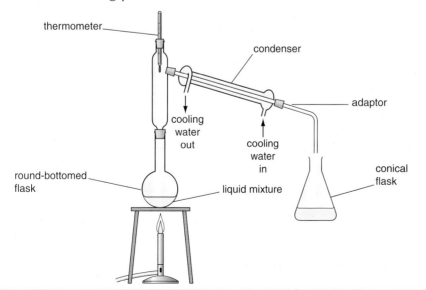

thermometer

condenser

cooling water out

cooling water in

adaptor

round-bottomed flask

liquid mixture

conical flask

exam tip

★ Make sure you can recognise CH_4 and C_2H_6, for example, as alkanes.

exam tip

★ Be sure to know the difference between **distillation** and **fractional distillation**.

■ Distillation – the mixture is heated to a particular temperature, one of the liquids evaporates and the heated vapour condenses and is collected

Fuels

Some properties of hydrocarbons, such as **viscosity**, **flammability** and **boiling point**, depend on the size of their molecules. These properties influence how hydrocarbons are used as **fuels**.

Note these points from the table:

- each fraction has a range of molecule sizes and a range of boiling points;
- the boiling points increase as the molecules get bigger;
- this could lead to a **hypothesis**, such as boiling point is related to molecule size – a graph would show the **correlation** better.

exam tip

★ You don't need to learn the names in the table, but you need to be able to compare data and information about the properties of fuels.

Fractions from an oil refinery					
Fraction	**Number of carbon atoms in molecule**	**Description and viscosity**	**Flammability**	**Boiling point (°C)**	**Uses**
Refinery gas	1–4	Colourless gases	Explodes if mixed with air and lit	Less than 40	Used as a fuel in the refinery Bottled and sold as liquefied petroleum gas
Naphtha	5–10	Yellowish liquid, flows very easily	Evaporates easily, vapour mixed with air is explosive	25–175	Petrol
Kerosene	10–14	Yellowish liquid, flows like water	Will burn when heated	150–260	Aircraft fuel
Light gas oil	14–20	Yellow liquid, thicker than water	Needs soaking onto a wick or other material to burn	235–360	Diesel fuel
Heavy gas oil	20–50	Yellow-brown liquid	Just burns when soaked onto a wick – very smoky	330–380	Used in the catalytic cracker (see page 58)
Fuel oil	60–80	Thick brown, sticky liquid	Needs to be hot and soaked onto a wick before it will burn	Above 490	Fuel oil for power stations and ships

check your understanding

22 Which of the following is **not** a mixture? *(1 mark)*

    A sea water   B air   C crude oil   D salt

23 What is similar about the molecules in a crude oil fraction? *(2 marks)*

24 Which of these is **not** a hydrocarbon? *(1 mark)*

    A CH_4 B C_2H_5OH C CH_3CH_3 D C_2H_6

25 What properties of crude oil fractions are related to molecule size, and how do they change as the molecules become larger? *(4 marks)*

Burning fuels

● Products of combustion

We need to burn fuels to give us energy, but there are other products of **combustion**.

- Most fuels are hydrocarbons and so contain carbon and hydrogen. Some fuels also contain some sulfur.
- So the gases released into the atmosphere when a fuel burns may include carbon dioxide, water (vapour), carbon monoxide and sulfur dioxide.

We can test the products formed when a hydrocarbon burns by using this apparatus. The water vapour **condenses** in the cold U-tube and the carbon dioxide turns the **limewater milky**.

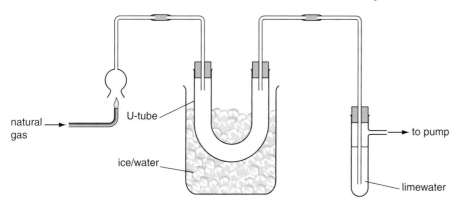

natural gas — U-tube — ice/water — to pump — limewater

■ Hydrocarbons burn to produce water and carbon dioxide as well as heat energy

The balanced equation for burning methane (used in most domestic central heating boilers) is:

$$CH_4 + 2O_2 \rightarrow CO_2 + 2H_2O$$

All pure alkanes produce just carbon dioxide and water when they burn in plenty of air (**complete combustion**).

● Harmful emissions from burning fuels

1 **Particles** (such as **soot** or **unburnt hydrocarbons**) may be released, especially if there is not enough oxygen for complete combustion (for example in a car engine). Particles cause **global dimming** – sunlight cannot get through the atmosphere as easily.
2 **Incomplete combustion** can also produce **carbon monoxide**, which is poisonous.
3 Sulfur impurities burn to produce sulfur dioxide. Sulfur dioxide causes **acid rain** – it dissolves in the water to produce sulfuric acid.
4 Carbon dioxide emissions cause **global warming** – due to an increased greenhouse effect.

Impact on the environment

What happens when we burn fossil fuels? The diagram says it all.

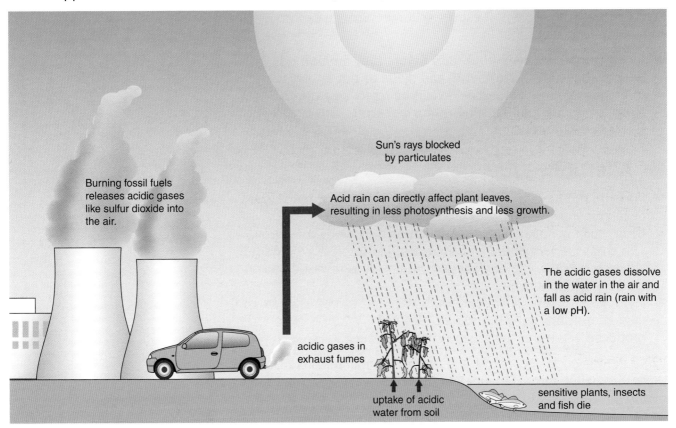

Sun's rays blocked
by particulates

Burning fossil fuels
releases acidic gases
like sulfur dioxide into
the air.

Acid rain can directly affect plant leaves,
resulting in less photosynthesis and less growth.

The acidic gases dissolve
in the water in the air and
fall as acid rain (rain with
a low pH).

acidic gases in
exhaust fumes

uptake of acidic
water from soil

sensitive plants, insects
and fish die

■ The environmental impacts of burning fossil fuels

Most scientists agree that the **data** show global warming is due to increased carbon dioxide emissions. **Opinions** about other social, economic and environmental impacts of the uses of fuels could be influenced by **bias** or political or economic needs.

check your understanding

㉖ Write the balanced chemical equation for pentane (C_5H_{12}) burning in excess air.   *(2 marks)*

㉗ Explain why two of the products of combustion could have opposite effects on global temperatures.   *(4 marks)*

㉘ The impurity in fossil fuels that causes air pollution is: *(1 mark)*

A silicone.   B silicon.   C silver.   D sulfur.

㉙ Which of the following is the correct word equation for the complete combustion of methane?
     (1 mark)

A methane + oxygen → carbon dioxide + water
B methane + water   → carbon dioxide + oxygen
C methane + oxygen → carbon dioxide + hydrogen
D methane + oxygen → carbon dioxide

Cleaner fuels

Sulfur in fuel is a problem. It causes **acid rain**. But we can do something to prevent that.

- Sulfur can be removed from fuels **before** they are burned. So we now have low-sulfur petrol and diesel to put in our cars.
- In power stations, sulfur dioxide can be removed from the waste gases **after** combustion, using quicklime. This is called **flue gas desulfurisation**.

● Alternative fuels

- Fuels do not have to come from crude oil. Plants, rubbish and even cow dung are used to produce **biofuels**.
- Crops such as sugar cane **absorb** carbon dioxide as they grow. The crops are **fermented** and then **distilled** to produce **ethanol**. When this burns, the original carbon dioxide is released and water is also produced.
- **Hydrogen** is made by splitting up water, and can be used in an engine or in **fuel cells** to produce electricity. Water is also produced whenever hydrogen is used as a fuel.

What are the social, economic and environmental impacts of using these alternative fuels? Ethanol and hydrogen have advantages over hydrocarbons as fuels:

- they do not deplete **non-renewable** crude oil reserves;
- they are 'clean' – they produce no toxic fumes, and using hydrogen to generate electricity does not produce carbon dioxide.

The drawback of ethanol is that it takes a lot of sugar cane to make the fuel – the fields could be used to produce food. Compared with Brazil, where a lot of ethanol is produced for fuel, Europe has less land available and a less sunny climate.

There is a problem with **storing** enough hydrogen as it is a gas and takes up a large volume. It needs to be pressurised or liquefied, which takes a lot of energy.

exam tip

★ If you're asked for economic and environmental effects of using fuels, you must remember to give a **balanced** argument and deal with **all** the aspects asked for – forget one, and you will lose half your marks.

■ Do you think these people are right? Are alternative cleaner fuels the whole answer?

● Energy outputs

The trouble with some cleaner fuels is that they do not give out as much energy as the dirty ones. Look at the table and decide which one you would like to put in your petrol tank. Which one will take you the furthest?

	Diesel	Biodiesel	Ethanol	Hydrogen (liquid)
Energy content per gallon (British thermal units)	130 000	120 000	80 000	30 500

check your understanding

③⓪ Describe two ways in which sulfur emissions from fuels can be reduced. *(2 marks)*

③① List two advantages and two disadvantages of using ethanol as a fuel. *(4 marks)*

③② For the combustion of ethanol (C_2H_5OH), write:
  a) the word equation; *(2 marks)*
  b) the balanced chemical equation. *(2 marks)*

③③ In Brazil, many cars are powered by ethanol. Ethanol is a fuel made from: *(1 mark)*

A   coal.
B   water.
C   plants.
D   yeast.

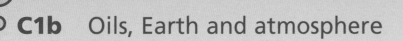

Cracking crude oil

- To make them more useful, the hydrocarbons from **fractional distillation** of crude oil can be broken down (**cracked**) to produce smaller molecules.
- **Cracking** involves heating the hydrocarbons to vaporise them and passing the vapours over a hot **catalyst**.
- A catalyst speeds up a reaction but is not consumed (used up by the reaction).
- Cracking involves **thermal decomposition** – using heat to break the molecules.

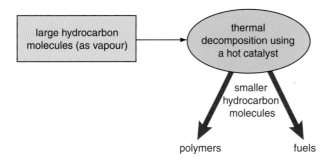

■ Cracking is the process that breaks large hydrocarbon molecules into smaller ones

The products of cracking include:

- **alkanes**, which are useful as fuels;
- **alkenes**, which are also used as fuels and as raw materials for plastics and chemicals.

● Alkenes

- **Alkenes**, such as ethene and propene, have the general formula C_nH_{2n}.
- **Alkenes** are **unsaturated hydrocarbons** containing **carbon–carbon double bonds**, shown in diagrams by C=C.
- 'Unsaturated' means that you can fit more hydrogen atoms into the molecule because of the carbon–carbon double bonds.
- Unsaturated hydrocarbon molecules can be represented in the following forms:

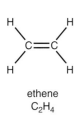

ethene
C_2H_4

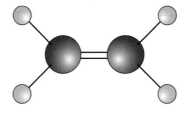

> **exam tip**
> ★ Make sure you can recognise C_2H_4 and C_3H_6, for example, as alkenes.

It is the C=C double bond that makes alkenes reactive and useful. The C=C bond also makes alkenes easy to detect – even in substances like margarine.

● The test for alkenes

Alkenes can be detected using **bromine or iodine water**.

You may have seen this with ethene gas (when you cracked an **alkane**) and/or with a vegetable oil like margarine (messy!).

To test for an alkene, you shake some bromine water with the suspect material. If it does contain an alkene then the **bromine water** is **decolorised** (the same goes for the **iodine solution**).

exam tip

★ When describing a colour change, make sure you say what the colour was to start with **and** what it is at the end. Bromine water starts brown/orange and becomes colourless. Iodine solution is either brown or purple and becomes colourless.

check your understanding

❶ Which **one** of the following sentences says the right thing about a catalyst? *(2 marks)*

  A A catalyst changes a reaction, but is not used up by the reaction.
  B A catalyst speeds up a reaction, but is not changed by the reaction.
  C A catalyst speeds up a reaction, but is not used up by the reaction.
  D A catalyst speeds up a reaction and is changed up by the reaction.

❷ Cracking hydrocarbons involves which type of reaction? *(1 mark)*

  A oxidation
  B reduction
  C neutralisation
  D decomposition

❸ Describe how margarine will react with iodine solution. *(2 marks)*

❹ Draw a diagram of an ethene molecule. Make sure you show all the bonds. *(2 marks)*

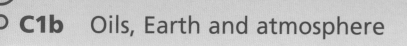

Making ethanol

We've already seen that the alkane fuels are often thought to be 'dirty' – they produce pollutants. **Ethanol** is a much 'cleaner' fuel to use in car engines – it burns to produce **water** and **carbon dioxide** only. There are no particulates and no sulfur dioxide.

● Ethanol from ethene

- **Ethene** is an alkene produced by cracking the heavier fractions in crude oil.
- Ethene can be reacted with **steam** at high temperature and pressure in the presence of a catalyst to produce ethanol.

$$C_2H_4 \quad + \quad H_2O \quad \xrightarrow[\text{high pressure}]{\text{catalyst}} \quad C_2H_5OH$$

ethene   steam   ethanol

Only 5% of the ethene is converted, but by recycling it through the reactor 95% conversion is eventually achieved. The ethanol has to be separated from the water by fractional distillation.

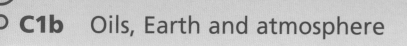

■ Water (steam) adds to ethene to make ethanol

● Ethanol by fermentation

- The process starts with a starchy material such as barley or, in hot countries like Brazil, sugar cane.
- The starch is extracted from the plants using hot water.
- It is then broken down into sugars by fermentation.
- The ethanol has to be concentrated and separated from the mixture by fractional distillation.

● Which process is best?

Using ethanol in car engines may produce less pollution than using petrol (see page 56), but is it better for us to use ethene (from crude oil) or fermentation of plant material to make ethanol for use as a fuel?

Look at the table at the top of page 61 of **some** of the advantages and disadvantages of each process.

	Advantages	Disadvantages
Ethanol from ethene	95% conversion One-stage process	Ethene comes from crude oil – a non-renewable resource High energy cost of temperature and pressure
Ethanol from fermentation	Cheap raw material Renewable plant material – conserves fossil fuels Low-cost process, as low temperature	15% mixture must be concentrated and purified by distillation – extra cost Two-stage process

You could be asked to analyse similar information to describe similarities and differences in:

- cost;
- speed of production;
- the raw material;
- the concentration of the ethanol produced;
- whether the process can be made continuous, or if you have to wait for a batch to finish.

check your understanding

5 Explain how you can separate the ethanol from the fermentation mixture. *(2 marks)*

6 Ethanol is purified by: *(1 mark)*

    A fractional distillation.
    B filtration.
    C crystallisation.
    D fermentation.

7 Ethene is produced from crude oil by: *(1 mark)*

    A thermal decomposition.
    B catalytic decomposition.
    C distillation and cracking.
    D fermentation and distillation.

Making polymers

exam tip

★ You don't need to learn the details of these diagrams, just to be able to interpret them. But make sure you can recognise the monomer molecules for ethene (C_2H_4) and propene (C_3H_6), and can draw the polymer if you are given the monomer.

- **Polymers** are extremely long molecules or chain molecules.
- In **polymerisation** reactions, many small molecules (**monomers**) join together to form very large molecules (**polymers**).
- **Plastics** are polymers and can be made from alkenes. The double bond in alkene monomers opens up to link to other monomers.

● Polymerisation

For example, ethene molecules join up to make **poly(ethene)** and propene molecules join up to make **poly(propene)**.

double bonds open and link the molecules together

expanded CH_3 looks like this:

many ethene monomers → polyethene

■ Poly(ethene) is a long-chain polymer molecule

many propene monomers → poly(propene)

■ Poly(propene) is a long-chain polymer molecule

● Properties of polymers

Poly(ethene) is an example of a **thermoplastic**. Thermoplastics can easily be softened by heat and moulded into shape. They have a low melting point because the weak intermolecular forces between the polymer chains are easily broken.

Thermosetting plastics are harder and less flexible than thermoplastics. They do not soften when heated, because of strong bonds linking the chains together. The plastic sets hard permanently – it can't be remoulded.

● Designing different polymers

The **properties** of polymers depend on the materials they are made from and the conditions (such as temperature, pressure, catalyst) under which they are made.

For example:

- **Slime** with different **viscosities** can be made from poly(ethenol) by adding different amounts of borax – the more borax added, the more solid it becomes.

- Poly(ethene) comes in two forms – high-density and low-density – made at different pressures or with different catalysts.
- PVC – real name poly(chloroethene) – is rigid but can be modified to make softer, more flexible forms by adding small 'plasticiser' molecules to the polymer.

New polymers are being developed using these methods. Most new materials are researched in the laboratory and the effect of changing different variables is investigated.

Here are some examples of new polymers made with special properties:

- **Smart polymers** respond to changes in their surroundings such as light or temperature – smart packaging materials could change colour when the temperature rises.
- **Hydrogels** are polymer gels that grow or shrink when water is added – they are used in wound dressings and nappies.
- **Shape-memory polymers** can stretch, but return to their original shape when heated.
- Waterproof coatings such as Gore-Tex® are actually layers of polymers designed with tiny holes that let through water vapour (sweat), but not liquid water.

■ A low-density poly(ethene) bottle will float, even when full of water, but the high-density lid sinks. Try it!

● Crude oil – too valuable to burn?

Some people say this. They believe the limited supply of crude oil should be reserved for making **useful products** rather than as **energy sources**.

Can you evaluate (work out) the social and economic advantages and disadvantages of using products from **crude oil** as **fuels** or as **raw materials** for plastic and other chemicals?

There's more about this in the next section.

check your understanding

8 Polymers are often plastics. Name the plastic that can be made from propene. *(1 mark)*

9 Match up the words A–D to numbers 1–4 in the following: *(4 marks)*

Polymers can be made from _____1_____. In these reactions, many small molecules (____2____) join together to form very ___3___ molecules (polymers). For example, ___4___ molecules join up to make poly(ethene).

A large   B monomers   C ethene   D alkenes

10 The properties of polymers depend on: *(1 mark)*

A   their colour and shape.
B   when they were invented.
C   how they were made.
D   what they are used for.

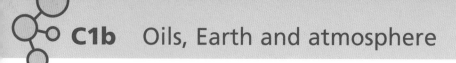

Waste-disposal problems

Most polymers are **non-biodegradable**, so they are not broken down (**decomposed**) by microorganisms, and this can lead to problems with waste disposal.

A solution to the problem would be to make **biodegradable** carrier bags and food wrapping. The problem is in developing a new polymer to last as long as it is needed before it rots away.

● What happens to non-biodegradable polymer waste?

Polymer waste can be disposed of in three ways:

- ● landfill;
- ● recycling;
- ● incinerator.

● Does it matter anyway?

Let's try to evaluate the social, economic and environmental impacts of the uses, disposal and recycling of polymers.

Here's some information for you to consider:

- ● In New York City alone, one less bag per person per year would save $250 000 in disposal costs.
- ● When 1 tonne of plastic bags is re-used or recycled, the energy equivalent of 11 barrels of oil is saved.
- ● Experts estimate that 500 billion to 1 trillion plastic bags are consumed and discarded annually worldwide – more than a million per minute.

Tables are useful tools when it comes to looking at lots of information together. The one on page 65 has just a few ideas for you.

Learn the **evaluation** technique:

- ● What are the pros and cons?
- ● Use the information provided, but check for the views of people who might be biased.
- ● Use the evidence of data in graphs or tables to support your argument.
- ● Come to your conclusion.

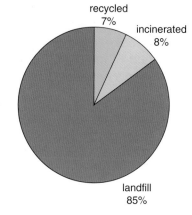

recycled 7%
incinerated 8%
landfill 85%

■ Most plastic waste ends up in the ground

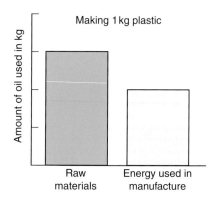

Making 1 kg plastic
Amount of oil used in kg
Raw materials
Energy used in manufacture

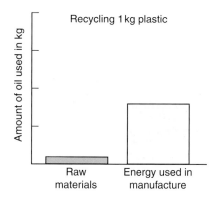

Recycling 1 kg plastic
Amount of oil used in kg
Raw materials
Energy used in manufacture

■ Recycling plastic saves oil resources, both as raw materials and as energy used in manufacturing

	Social	Economic	Environmental
Uses of polymers	Many products are made of polymers, e.g. sports equipment, clothing, fashion, sporting, everyday wear Food packaging ICT and high-tech items The list is endless ...	Creates employment: - manufacture - sales - disposal - product design The list is as long as your imagination	Uses fossil fuel (oil) as raw material Manufacture may produce toxic waste Creates non-biodegradable waste at end of useful life
Disposal of polymers	Unpleasant to live close by	Creates employment: - refuse collectors - landfill/incinerator workers	Landfill uses valuable land Landfill is unsightly Incineration produces a lot of ash, greenhouse gases and toxic fumes, but can also be used to generate energy
Recycling of polymers	Happy communities because their environment is cleaner But there is effort involved in individuals having to sort domestic waste	Creates employment Is recycled plastic more expensive than new plastic?	Saves valuable raw material Produces much less pollution Reduces use of landfill sites Uses energy, possibly more than the energy needed to make new plastic

check your understanding

⓫ Recycling supermarket carrier bags is good for the environment because: *(1 mark)*

    A it saves money.
    B it saves crude oil.
    C it creates jobs.
    D it saves arguing about it.

⓬ Using the information on this page, evaluate the social and economic advantages and disadvantages of using products from crude oil as fuels, or as raw materials for plastic and other chemicals. *(6 marks)*

exam tip

★ If you're asked to **evaluate** the information supplied, you must remember to give a **balanced** argument and deal with **the evidence for and against** – forget one and you will lose marks.

Vegetable oils and fuels

Vegetable oils are important **foods** and **fuels**; they provide **energy**.

● Vegetable oils in food

- ● Vegetable oils provide energy and also **nutrients,** such as essential fatty acids and vitamin E.
- ● Frying food in oil adds flavour and enables a high temperature to be reached – food cooks faster.
- ● Vegetable oils are extracted from some fruits, seeds and nuts.
- ● This **extraction** is done by crushing the plant material and removing the oil by **pressing** or in some cases by **distillation.** Then water and other impurities are removed.
- ● Vegetable oils that are **unsaturated** contain carbon–carbon double bonds. These can be detected by reacting with **bromine** or **iodine water.**

● Turning plant oils into margarine

- ● Vegetable oils that are unsaturated can be hardened by reacting them with hydrogen in the presence of a nickel catalyst at about 60 °C. This is called **hydrogenation.**
- ● This is part of the process of making margarine.
- ● The **hydrogenated** oils have higher melting points so they are solids at room temperature, making them useful as spreads and in cakes and pastries.

Some people say that margarine is better for you than butter. Can you use the data in the table to evaluate the effects of using vegetable oils in foods and the impacts on diet and health? (Calculate the **total** amount of saturated fat in 100 g of the margarine.)

Plant oil	Where oil is stored in the plant
Olive oil	Fruit
Rape oil	Seeds
Peanut oil	Nut (food store for seeds)
Avocado oil	Fruit
Sunflower oil	Seed
Palm oil	Fruit

■ Some common plant oils and the sources of the oil

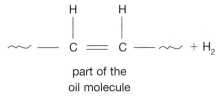

part of the oil molecule

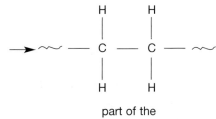

part of the margarine molecule

Comparing butter and different margarines			
	Butter	**Hard margarine**	**Soft margarine made with olive oil**
Fat per 100 g/g	81	81	59
of which saturates/%	64	20	24
Cholesterol per serving/mg	30	0	0

Remember that:

- ● too much dietary fat and not enough exercise can lead to obesity;
- ● saturated fats can lead to heart disease and stroke;
- ● the ingredients label may also show other additives that have other effects on health (salt, cholesterol-lowering).

exam tip

★ You don't need to remember the summary table – but you may be asked to analyse similar information in the exam and sort it out into headings like these.

Vegetable oils for fuels – biodiesel

It's true! Old oil from the chip shop can be used to make fuel. But most **biodiesel** is made from crops grown for that purpose. Biodiesel is renewable and conserves crude oil reserves.

But, as well as benefits, there are drawbacks and risks of using vegetable oils to produce fuels.

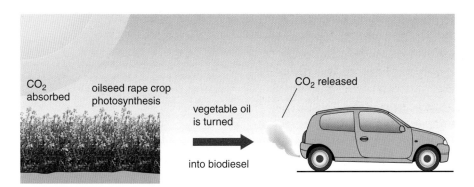

CO_2 absorbed

oilseed rape crop photosynthesis

vegetable oil is turned

CO_2 released

into biodiesel

■ Burning biodiesel produces no CO_2 overall; CO_2 is absorbed by the plants from which the fuel is made

Benefits	Drawbacks	Risks
No modification of diesel engine needed	A lot of land is used to grow plants for fuel instead of food	Increased use of fertilisers
Can be mixed with ordinary diesel		Increased use of GM crops to withstand weedkillers (see page 29)
Much **less polluting** than ordinary diesel		Allergic reactions to chemicals used in the whole process
It **biodegrades** faster than ordinary diesel		
It is **carbon-neutral**		
Biodiesel can be produced locally – local economic benefit		

check your understanding

⑬ **a)** What is an unsaturated oil? *(1 mark)*
   b) Describe how to test butter and a range of oils to see which is unsaturated. *(2 marks)*
   c) Explain why unsaturated fats are considered to be healthier. *(2 marks)*
   d) Give the steps needed to turn an unsaturated fat into a form useful for baking. *(3 marks)*

⑭ What is most biodiesel made from? *(1 mark)*

⑮ The reaction to form solid fats from liquid oils is called: *(1 mark)*

   A distillation.   B polymerisation.   C cracking.   D hydrogenation.

⑯ Biodiesel is carbon-neutral. That means: *(1 mark)*

   A it does not produce soot when it burns.
   B the exhaust gases have a pH of 7.
   C the exhaust carbon dioxide is neutral.
   D it produces the same amount of CO_2 as was absorbed by the plants from which it was made.

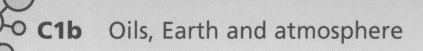

Food additives and emulsifiers

● Do you know what you are eating?

1 Colours, flavours and stability are often changed by processing food.

2 Processed foods may contain **additives** to improve:
- appearance – pink ice cream gets you ready to taste strawberries;
- taste – we all add salt (just a little) to our fish and chips;
- shelf-life – food that's gone off in the back of the fridge is a nasty shock.

3 The European Union says that additives must be listed in the ingredients so we know what we are eating. Additives permitted in the EU have **E-numbers** to show they passed safety tests.

4 Even natural substances used as additives have E-numbers: vitamin C is E300.

● Emulsifiers in food

- **Oils** do not **dissolve** in water but they can be used to produce **emulsions**.
- **Emulsions** are special **mixtures** of oil and water that are thicker than oil or water – they have a higher **viscosity**.
- **Emulsions** provide better texture, coating ability and appearance than oil or water separately. That means they taste better in the mouth, stick to the food and look more appetising than just oil and water.
- Salad dressings (such as mayonnaise) and ice creams are emulsions.
- **Emulsifiers** stop the oil and water mixture separating out. In mayonnaise the emulsifier is egg yolk. French salad dressing (olive oil and vinegar) has no emulsifier and you can watch the two separate just after you've shaken them up.

● Food analysis

Chemical analysis can be used to identify additives in foods.

One way of detecting **artificial colours** is **chromatography**. You will probably have done this with inks – from bottles or using the tips of felt pens. You may have used food colourings or even the colours from Smarties™.

In analytical laboratories a more **sensitive, reliable** and **accurate** type of chromatography is used. These tests can show the presence of illegal additives.

■ Emulsifiers keep emulsions emulsified

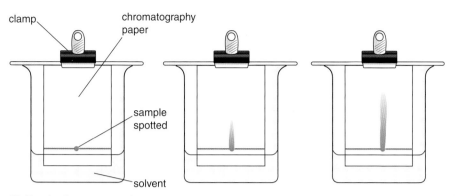

clamp

chromatography paper

sample spotted

solvent

■ Simple chromatography

Are food additives safe to eat?

E-numbers are supposed to be safe. But we've all heard of people (maybe a friend or yourself) who are allergic to a **colouring**, **flavouring** or **preservative**.

So while there are **benefits**, there are also **drawbacks** and **risks** involved in using additives.

check your understanding

⑰ If a food additive has an E-number it means that it has passed: *(1 mark)*

  A safety tests.
  B effectiveness tests.
  C a board of enquiry.
  D an exam.

⑱ Chromatography can be used to detect: *(1 mark)*

  A colourings.
  B artificial flavourings.
  C colourings and flavours.
  D colourings, flavours and preservatives.

⑲ Emulsions without emulsifiers: *(1 mark)*

  A are not real emulsions.
  B separate quickly.
  C go bad too soon.
  D have no oil in them.

The Earth and continental drift

● The structure of the Earth

The Earth consists of a **core**, **mantle** and **crust**.

- The **inner core** is solid, the **outer core** is liquid.
- The **mantle** is a thick band of mostly solid rock, but it can flow very slowly.
- The **crust** is much thinner than the mantle and core.

Scientists once thought that:

- as the Earth had cooled down it contracted;
- the shrinking of the crust caused wrinkling on the surface;
- this wrinkling is seen as mountains, valleys, volcanoes, etc.

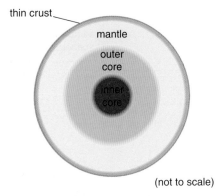

■ A section through the Earth

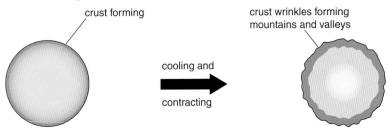

■ Early ideas about the formation of mountains and valleys on the Earth's surface

Then a meteorologist named Alfred Wegener came up with a radically different idea.

● Continental drift

Wegener observed that on opposite sides of the Atlantic Ocean there were:

- similar ancient rocks and mountain chains;
- very similar fossils;
- a very good fit of the shape of the coastlines.

He said this could be explained if:

- all the continents were once joined together as one supercontinent;
- the supercontinent broke up and the continents had slowly moved apart.

But Wegener's theory of crustal movement (**continental drift**) was not generally accepted for many years after it was proposed:

- other scientists were hostile – after all, it had been proposed by a weatherman, not a geologist;
- the geological experts had other interpretations of some of the evidence – a bridge of land between the continents could have allowed animals to pass freely;

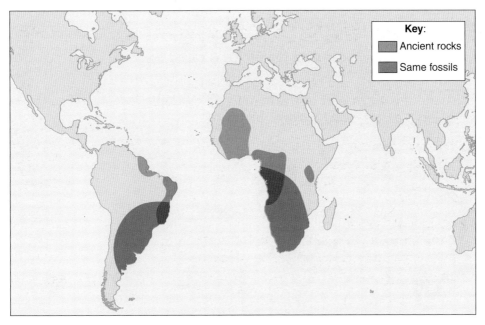

■ The 'jigsaw fit' and similar rock types and fossils of South America and Africa were used as evidence for Wegener's theory of continental drift

- Wegener could not explain how the continents could move through the solid ocean floor;
- nobody knew what was at the bottom of the oceans between the continents.

Today, scientists accept Wegener's theory because of new evidence about the ocean floor, and new evidence about the interior of the Earth and a theory to explain how the crust can move (see page 72). This is an example of how scientific ideas can change with time as scientists check each other's ideas and evidence.

check your understanding

20 Draw a labelled diagram clearly showing the structure of the Earth. *(4 marks)*

21 Describe how a new scientific theory becomes accepted by other scientists. *(2 marks)*

22 Mountains and valleys on the Earth's surface were once thought to be the result of: *(1 mark)*

    A the Earth getting old and becoming wrinkly.
    B the Earth drying out like a prune.
    C the Earth cooling and shrinking.
    D giant creatures in the Earth's core pushing up the rocks.

23 Which one of the following pieces of evidence cannot be explained using Wegener's theory of continental drift? *(1 mark)*

    A Different continents have fossils of the same extinct creatures.
    B There are deep rift valleys in the middle of the oceans.
    C The close fit of the coastlines of the continents.
    D Similar rocks appear on continents either side of the Atlantic Ocean.

Plate tectonics

The theory that replaced continental drift in the 1970s is called the **theory of plate tectonics**. This theory says:

● The Earth's crust and the upper part of the mantle are cracked into a number of large pieces called **tectonic plates**.

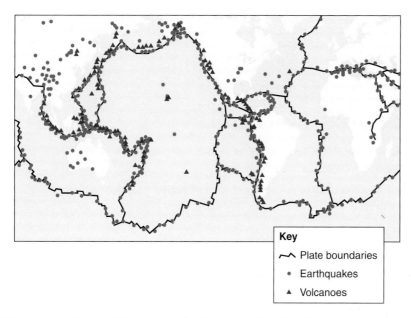

Key

⌁ Plate boundaries

• Earthquakes

▲ Volcanoes

■ The tectonic plates and the pattern of volcanoes and earthquakes

● **Natural radioactive** processes deep inside the Earth produce heat – just like in nuclear reactors.
● This heat causes **convection currents** within the mantle, even though it is mostly solid.
● The tectonic plates move because of the convection currents.

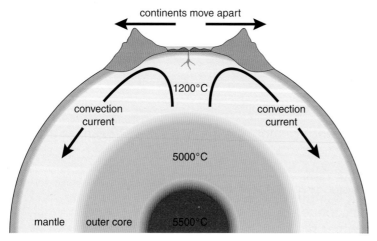

continents move apart

1200°C

convection current

convection current

5000°C

mantle   outer core   5500°C

■ Convection currents make tectonic plates move

Earthquakes and volcanoes

- Usually the **tectonic plates** move really slowly – only a few centimetres a year.
- The movement causes stresses and strains to build up between the plates.
- These stresses and strains can be released by sudden and disastrous movements of the tectonic plates.
- **Earthquakes** and/or **volcanic eruptions** occur at the boundaries between **tectonic plates** as the result of sudden **tectonic plate** movement.

Where, but not when

- Plate tectonic theory predicts **where** earthquakes and volcanic eruptions will occur.
- But scientists cannot accurately predict **when** stresses and strains will be released, and so cannot predict when earthquakes and volcanic eruptions will occur.

They can measure:

- the forces in rocks;
- tiny movements and bulges in the Earth's crust;
- shock waves from small earthquakes that happen before the main one;
- movement of the tectonic plates using global positioning systems.

These may give a **warning sign** that an earthquake or eruption is **likely**, but not a definite prediction of when.

check your understanding

24 Tectonic plates are in which part of the Earth? *(1 mark)*

- A the crust and mantle
- B the mantle and core
- C the outer core
- D the inner core

25 Tectonic plates move because of: *(1 mark)*

- A conduction
- B convection
- C radiation
- D pressure

26 Where and why do earthquakes occur? *(2 marks)*

Gases in the atmosphere

Mainly nitrogen and oxygen

For 200 million years, the proportions of different gases in the **atmosphere** have been much the same as they are today:

- about four-fifths (80%) **nitrogen**;
- about one-fifth (20%) **oxygen**;
- small proportions of various other gases, including **carbon dioxide**, **water vapour** and **noble gases**.

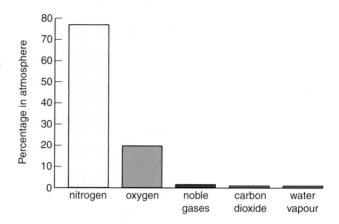

■ The gases in our atmosphere

The noble gases

(Not posh – just unreactive!)

The **noble gases** are in Group 0 of the Periodic Table. That's the column on the right-hand side with helium at the top.

There's very little of them in the atmosphere, but they are really useful in some situations, for example:

- **filament lamps**;
- **electric discharge tubes** (neon lights).

That's because they are all chemically **unreactive** and therefore do not react with other materials, even at high temperatures. (The tungsten filament of a light bulb lasts less than a second in air, but stays bright for many hours in argon.)

Helium is much less dense than air. Therefore it is used in balloons – for parties, carnivals and even scientific experiments high in the atmosphere.

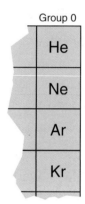

Group 0
He
Ne
Ar
Kr

■ The position of the noble gases in the Periodic Table

■ Helium balloons rise because they are less dense than air

exam tip

★ Remember to be precise in what you write: a lot of people say helium is 'lighter than air', but a tonne of helium weighs the same as a tonne of air. You must say it is 'less dense than air'.

Carbon dioxide in the atmosphere today

- There are processes that add CO_2 to the atmosphere and those that remove it.
- But there is evidence that levels of **carbon dioxide** in the atmosphere are increasing.
- Burning **fossil fuels** (to produce energy) adds CO_2 to the atmosphere.
- There is a **correlation** between the sudden increase in CO_2 levels and the beginning of the Industrial Revolution.
- This increase in CO_2 is thought to be causing global warming.

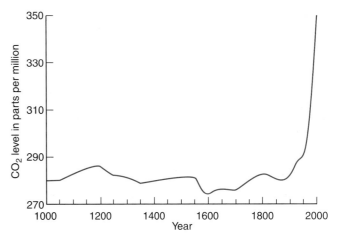

■ The amount of carbon dioxide in the atmosphere has increased over the past 1000 years – note the rapid rise since about 1860

check your understanding

Atmospheric CO₂ since 1750	Year					
	1750	1800	1850	1900	1950	2000
Concentration of carbon dioxide in the atmosphere/% by volume	0.0278	0.0282	0.0288	0.0297	0.0310	0.0368

27 **a)** Use the data in the table to calculate the percentage change of carbon dioxide levels in the atmosphere since 1750. *(2 marks)*
  b) Suggest two possible reasons for the rise levels of carbon dioxide in this time. *(2 marks)*

28 The proportions of nitrogen and oxygen in the atmosphere are, respectively: *(1 mark)*

  A 20 and 80%.
  B 30 and 70%.
  C 70 and 30%.
  D 80 and 20%.

29 Argon is used in filament lamps because: *(1 mark)*

  A it is cheap.
  B it is colourless.
  C it does not react with the filament.
  D it does not matter what is used.

Theories about the atmosphere

● Where did it come from?

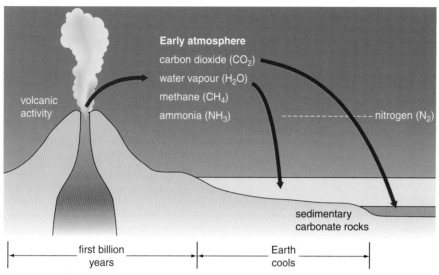

Early atmosphere
carbon dioxide (CO_2)
water vapour (H_2O)
methane (CH_4)
ammonia (NH_3) ------------------ nitrogen (N_2)

volcanic activity

sedimentary carbonate rocks

|←— first billion years —→|←— Earth cools —→|

■ Volcanoes released the gases in the Earth's early atmosphere

During the first billion years of the Earth's existence, there was intense **volcanic activity**.

Volcanoes released the gases that formed the early atmosphere:

● carbon dioxide (CO_2) – main component of the early atmosphere;
● methane (CH_4) – small proportion;
● ammonia (NH_3) – small proportion;
● water vapour (H_2O).

As the Earth cooled, the water vapour condensed to form the oceans.

Later, ammonia reacted with oxygen to produce nitrogen.

● Notice that, during this early period, the Earth's atmosphere was mainly carbon dioxide and there would have been little or no oxygen gas.
● This would have been like the atmospheres of **Mars** and **Venus** today.
● Over time, nitrogen increased, carbon dioxide decreased and oxygen increased.

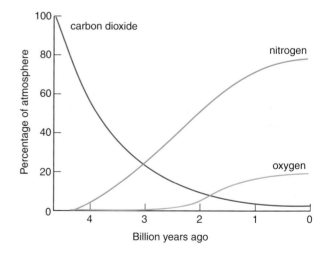

■ How the composition of the Earth's atmosphere has changed

Alternative theories about the atmosphere

There are different theories about the proportions of these gases in the early atmosphere. These theories are hard to test, as there is no direct evidence.

Some theories suggest that the source of water was **comets**, not volcanoes.

Explaining the change in carbon dioxide and oxygen levels

- Volcanoes add CO_2 to the atmosphere.
- Sea water reacts with and removes CO_2 from the atmosphere.
- Plants (through **photosynthesis**) also remove CO_2 from the atmosphere.
- As plants developed 3 billion years ago, carbon dioxide levels began to fall and oxygen levels began to rise.

Most of the carbon from the carbon dioxide in the air gradually became locked up in sedimentary rocks as **carbonates** and fossil fuels.

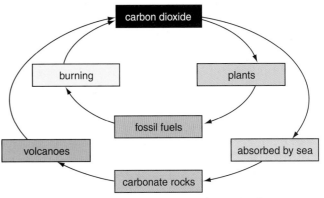

■ Carbon dioxide moves into and out of the atmosphere

check your understanding

30 Describe how the proportions of oxygen and carbon dioxide in the Earth's atmosphere have changed over the past 4 billion years. *(4 marks)*

31 Carbon dioxide levels in the atmosphere have risen over the past 200 years, and this may be causing global warming. Explain why the natural processes that greatly reduced carbon dioxide levels in the Earth's early atmosphere will not be able to remove the extra carbon dioxide by the twenty-second century and solve the global warming problem. *(2 marks)*

32 The early atmosphere was like the current atmosphere of which two planets? *(1 mark)*

    A Mercury and Mars
    B Mercury and Venus
    C Mars and Venus
    D Venus and Saturn

Thermal radiation

● Infra-red and thermal radiation

- When a body **absorbs** any type of electromagnetic radiation it gets hotter. Absorbing infra-red radiation gives the most obvious heating effect. **Infra-red radiation** is often called **thermal radiation** or heat. They are the same thing.
- In the picture, the hot element of the electric fire **emits** or radiates a lot of thermal radiation every second. The energy is transferred through the air by electromagnetic waves. The person in front of the fire feels warm because she absorbs some of this energy.
- Objects heat up (**increase temperature**) when they absorb thermal radiation faster than they emit it.
- All bodies transfer energy by thermal radiation. The hotter the body, the more energy it transfers (radiates) each second.

● All bodies absorb and emit thermal radiation

But some surfaces are better than others. The chart gives the difference between surfaces.

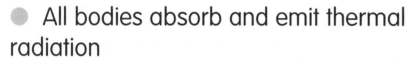

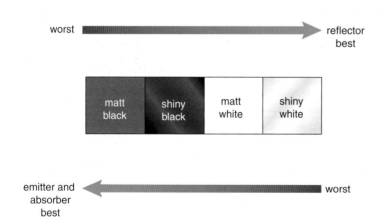

■ Shiny aluminium foil helps keep food hot for longer by reflecting thermal radiation emitted by the hot food back into the food

- Dark-coloured, matt surfaces absorb and emit thermal radiation faster than light-coloured, shiny surfaces.
- Good absorbers of thermal radiation are also good emitters of thermal radiation.
- Light-coloured, shiny surfaces are good reflectors of thermal radiation.
- Shiny surfaces reduce heat transfer by thermal radiation.

● Comparing surfaces

The picture on page 79 of the two different containers shows a simple way of comparing the effect of surface on the rate of absorption.

■ The silvered surface reflects thermal radiation, reducing the energy absorbed by the wine, keeping it cool for longer

- Repeating the experiment would always give the same result; this makes the results **reliable**.
- An **error** in reading the thermometer could give an **anomalous** result. An anomalous result is one that does not fit the pattern.
- Using a temperature sensor and data logger would increase the **accuracy** of the temperature measurements. This is because you are less likely to misread the value (giving a **random error**).
- Increasing the accuracy means that the recorded temperatures are closer to the **true temperature**.
- A temperature sensor is probably also more **precise** – it is more **sensitive** to small changes than a thermometer that only shows readings to 0.5 °C.

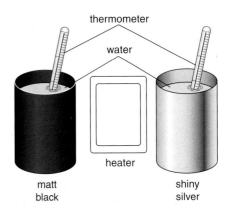

■ The temperature inside the black container goes up more quickly than the temperature inside the shiny silver container

check your understanding

1 Explain why a hot pie placed in a refrigerator cools down. *(2 marks)*

2 A hollow metal cube is filled with boiling water. Each side of the cube is a different colour or texture. The values in the table are taken with a thermal radiation detector facing each side of the cube. The higher the value, the greater the amount of thermal radiation emitted by the surface.
  a) Match each side (A–D) to one of the colours and textures in the list below. *(4 marks)*
  matt black   matt white   shiny black   shiny silver
  b) Why is it important in this experiment that the detector and meter were sensitive to small changes? *(1 mark)*

3 The graph shows how the temperature inside a room changes.
  a) At which point (X, Y or Z) is the room absorbing and emitting thermal radiation at the same rate? Give a reason for your answer. *(2 marks)*
  b) The temperature of the room continues to increase at the same rate for a further hour. What is the room temperature at 13.00 h? *(2 marks)*

Side	A	B	C	D
Detector value	0.37	0.72	0.76	0.26

exam tip

★ When the examiner asks you to 'explain' you should apply some logical thinking, for example, give the reasons for something happening in terms of theory.

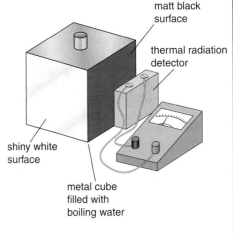

exam tip

★ You need to **extrapolate** the graph. This means continue drawing the line following the same pattern.

Conduction and convection

The transfer of thermal energy by **conduction** and **convection** involves the movement of particles.

● Conduction happens mainly in solids

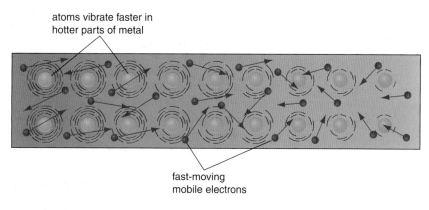

atoms vibrate faster in hotter parts of metal

fast-moving mobile electrons

- At the hot end of the conductor, thermal energy increases the **kinetic energy** of the atoms.
- The atoms **vibrate** more quickly and with bigger amplitude.
- These atoms collide with neighbouring atoms.
- The extra kinetic energy is passed from atom to atom.
- This is a slow process.

● Metals are better conductors than non-metals

- Metals have **electrons** that are free to move.
- These mobile electrons transfer energy rapidly.
- Non-metals have no mobile electrons, so conduct energy slowly.
- A poor conductor is a good **insulator**.

● Air is a good insulator

■ A polar bear has a thick fur coat. The fur traps small pockets of air. The air reduces the energy transferred by conduction, helping to keep the polar bear warm

Convection happens only in liquids and gases

Convection is the transfer of thermal energy by the movement of a liquid or gas due to differences in **density**.

- Air particles gain energy and move around more quickly.
- The particles move apart, taking up more space.
- The warm air **expands**, becoming **less dense** than the colder air above.
- The warmer air rises, pushing colder, denser air downwards.

A hot-water system uses convection

- A boiler heats the water.
- Hot, less dense water rises to the hot-water tank.
- Colder, denser water falls from the cold-water tank.
- A convection current circulates the water.

Question: 'When is a radiator not a radiator?'
Answer: 'When it's a radiator in a central heating system.'

The radiators in a central heating system are really convector heaters. By heating up the air, they create a convection current that transfers the energy around the room.

To transfer a lot of energy by radiation, they would need to be a lot hotter than they are. They would need to glow red hot.

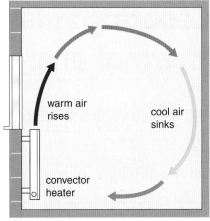

■ The heater creates an air flow called a **convection current**

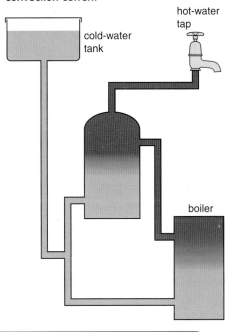

check your understanding

4 Greg and Jill pack an insulated picnic box with food. Greg wants to put the frozen ice pack at the bottom of the bag. Jill says it would be better if the ice pack were on top of the food at the top of the bag.

Where in the box should the ice pack go? Explain the reason for your answer. *(3 marks)*

exam tip

★ Write out the two correct statements. It will help you remember them.

5 Which **two** statements describe the transfer of thermal energy through water? *(2 marks)*

A Energy is transferred by electromagnetic waves.
B Energy transfer does not involve particles.
C Energy is transferred because the water expands.
D Energy is transferred by mobile electrons.
E Energy is transferred because the density of water changes as it is heated.

6 Explain why copper is a better thermal conductor than plastic. *(1 mark)*

Reducing rates of heat (thermal energy) transfer

● Different bodies transfer heat at different rates

The **rate** of transfer of heat to or from a body depends on:

- the material the body is made from;
- the shape and size of the body;
- the difference in temperature between the body and its surroundings.

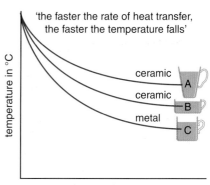

'the faster the rate of heat transfer, the faster the temperature falls'

temperature in °C

ceramic — A
ceramic — B
metal — C

time in minutes

Comparing graph lines	
A and C or B and C	The bigger the temperature difference between the water and the air, the faster the rate of heat transfer
A and C	A metal mug conducts heat away from the water more quickly than a ceramic mug
B and C	Increasing the surface area increases the rate of heat transfer

To make the comparison of these graphs a **fair test**:

- only the shape or material of the mug was changed (the **independent variable**);
- the volume and starting temperature of the water was kept the same (**control variables**).

● A vacuum flask keeps hot drinks hot and cold drinks cold

Heat transfer by conduction, convection and radiation is reduced by:

- the vacuum between the double glass walls (conduction and convection);
- the silvering on the glass walls (radiation);
- the plastic stopper (conduction and convection).

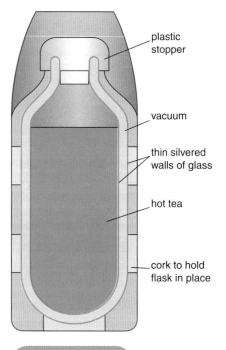

plastic stopper

vacuum

thin silvered walls of glass

hot tea

cork to hold flask in place

● Keeping your home warm is about reducing heat transfer

Most methods of **insulation** involve trapping **air**:

- air trapped in small pockets cannot move far, so heat transfer by convection is reduced;

exam tip

★ An exam question may not be about house insulation, but if it's about keeping warm, it's almost certainly about trapped air reducing heat loss by convection and conduction.

- air is a good insulator, so heat transfer by conduction is reduced.

Shiny materials, often in the loft or behind radiators, reflect heat, so reducing heat transfer by radiation.

Draught excluders help reduce the effect of convection currents pulling cold air into the house.

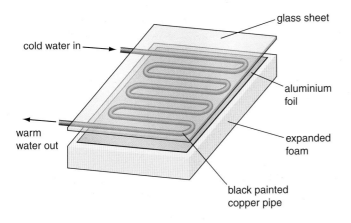

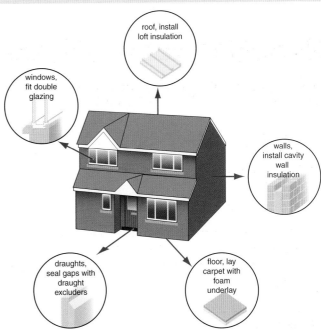

■ Heat transferred through the roof, walls, windows, floor and doors of a house can be reduced by using insulation

check your understanding

7 The diagram above shows a model solar water heater made by a student. Explain why each of the features labelled in the diagram has been included in the design. *(6 marks)*

8 Explain why woollen gloves keep your hands warm. *(2 marks)*

9 The *U*-values for different types of double glazing are given in the table. A lower *U*-value means less heat loss per second through the window. The gap between the glass, which can be 12 mm or 20 mm, is filled with either air or argon.

		U-value	
Data set	Glass type	12 mm gap	20 mm gap
1	Type A with air	2.9	2.8
2	Type A with argon	2.7	2.6
3	Type B with air	1.9	1.8
4	Type B with argon	1.6	1.5

> ## exam tip
> ★ You don't need to memorise anything about *U*-values.

a) Windows with a 20 mm gap cost more than those with a 12 mm gap. Is the extra expense worthwhile? Explain the reason for your answer. *(1 mark)*

b) The data were obtained with a temperature difference of 15 °C between one side of the window and the other. How would these figures change if the temperature difference increased to 20 °C? Give a reason for your answer. *(2 marks)*

c) Which sets of data should be compared in order to decide which type of glass, A or B, makes the most energy-efficient double-glazed window? *(1 mark)*

Energy efficiency

● You can't create energy from nothing; it's just impossible!

Energy can be:

- **transferred** (moved) from one place to another;
- **transformed** (changed) from one form into another.

Remember that energy cannot be created or destroyed.

● Energy makes things happen, but only when it's transformed

Chemical energy stored in fuels is useful only when a device transforms the energy into another form. A car engine transforms chemical energy to kinetic energy, heat and sound.

A **Sankey diagram** shows energy transformation. The wider the arrow, the greater is the percentage of energy transformed to that form. The Sankey diagram shows that the energy input and the total energy output are the same. The energy has been **conserved**. But not all output energy is **useful**. The heat and light is **wasted energy**.

An **efficient** device is good at transferring input energy into useful output energy.

$$\text{efficiency} = \frac{\text{useful energy transferred by the device}}{\text{total energy supplied to the device}}$$

- Energy is measured in **joules** (J).
- Efficiency has no unit.
- Efficiency is given as a decimal number or a percentage.

● Energy can never vanish

- All energy, useful and wasted, is eventually transferred to the surroundings, which become warmer.
- The energy shared between a lot of molecules becomes spread out.
- As the energy spreads out, it becomes more difficult to use for further energy transformations.
- The energy has not vanished – it's just not useful any more.

In some devices, energy normally wasted can be usefully used. On cold days the inside of a car is warmed by waste heat from the engine.

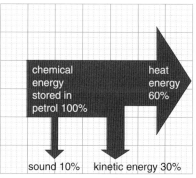

■ Sankey diagram for a petrol engine

exam tip

★ You do not need to remember this equation. But you do need to be able to use it and rearrange it.

Payback time is not the same as cost effectiveness

Payback time is the time it takes to recover the money spent reducing energy consumption from the money saved on energy bills. For example, £240 spent on loft insulation reduces the annual energy bill by £80. The payback time is 3 years.

How **cost effective** it is to reduce energy consumption depends on:

- initial cost;
- replacement time.

Method of reducing energy transfer	Cost to install/ £	Annual saving on energy bills/£	Replacement time/ years	Total saving over 5 years/£	Total saving over 20 years/£
Draught-proofing	75	25	5	$(5 \times 25) - 75$ $= 50$	(20×25) $- (4 \times 75)$ $= 200$
Temperature controls on radiators	120	20	20	$(5 \times 20) -$ $120 = -20$	(20×20) $- 120$ $= 280$

Draught-proofing has the shorter payback time (3 years), and over 5 years is the most cost effective. But over 20 years, draught-proofing must be replaced four times, so over 20 years the radiator controls are more cost effective.

check your understanding

⑩ The data in the table compare a filament lamp with the equivalent energy-efficient lamp.

	Filament lamp	Energy-efficient lamp
Average lifetime/hours	1000	8000
Cost to buy/£	0.70	2.20
Energy cost for 1000 hours use/£	6.00	1.50

Calculate the total saving a householder would make by replacing one filament lamp with an energy-efficient lamp. *(3 marks)*

⑪ A fluorescent light transforms 25% of the input energy to light and 75% to heat. Which **one** of the following does **not** happen to the output energy from the lamp? *(1 mark)*

A It becomes spread out.
C It stops existing.
B It makes the surrounding air warmer.
D It becomes more difficult to use for further energy transfers.

⑫ A TV is 65% efficient. Each second it is on, the useful energy output is 520 J.
a) Calculate the energy input to the TV each second that it is switched on. *(2 marks)*
b) When it is switched to standby, the energy input to the TV halves. Why should TVs be switched off rather than switched to standby? *(1 mark)*

⑬ A solar cell is 8% efficient. What is the energy output each second when the energy input to the panel is 2400 J each second? *(2 marks)*

A 33 J   B 192 J   C 300 J   D 19 200 J

Electrical power and energy costs

Electrical energy is easily transformed into other energy forms. This is what makes it so useful, and why so many devices are designed to work from an electricity supply. Examples are given in the table.

Energy input to device	Device	Useful energy output from device
Electrical	Loudspeaker, buzzer, bell	Sound
Electrical	Grill, toaster, fire, iron, kettle	Heat
Electrical	Lamp, computer screen, digital display	Light
Electrical	Motor	Kinetic
Electrical	Rechargeable battery, phone charger	Chemical

● Power

Power is the **rate at which a device transforms energy**. It is measured in **watts (W)**:

● 1 watt = 1 joule of energy transformed in one second (1 J/s);
● 1 kilowatt (kW) = 1000 watts (W).

The total electrical energy transformed by a device depends on:

● how long the device is used;
● the power of the device.

● Cost of the energy

The cost of using a device is calculated using **two** equations:

energy transferred   =   power   ×   time
(in kilowatt-hours, kWh)   (in kilowatts, kW)   (in hours, h)

total cost = number of kilowatt-hours × cost per kilowatt-hour

This is the **only** time that we calculate energy in kilowatt-hours.

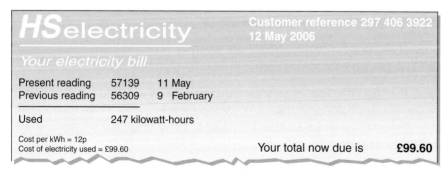

■ The readings on the electricity meter are used to calculate the total energy cost over 3 months

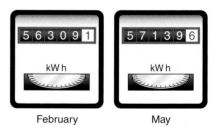

■ An electricity meter records the energy supplied in kilowatt-hours

Choosing the right device for the job

Different devices that do the same job may have particular advantages and disadvantages. For example, there are many different types of electric heater. Which one do you choose?

For a quick blast of heat in a garage, shed or kitchen, the fan heater would probably be first choice. To keep the chill out of a bedroom, it's probably the oil-filled radiator.

exam tip

★ If you are asked to compare different devices, describe similarities and differences. What is an advantage for one device will often be a disadvantage for the other.

Heater type	Advantages	Disadvantages
2.5 kW fan heater	Two power settings Rapidly warms a room Cheap to buy Small size	Expensive to run on full power for long Fan can be noisy Does not give same room temperature throughout
400 W oil-filled radiator	Low operating cost Makes no noise Maintains a steady room temperature	One power setting Takes time to warm up a room Expensive compared with other heaters Bulky

check your understanding

⑭ Calculate the cost of using a 1600 W hair dryer for 20 minutes each day, Monday to Saturday. One kilowatt-hour of energy costs 12 p. *(4 marks)*

⑮ How much energy does a 60 W filament lamp switched on for 2 hours transfer? *(2 marks)*

    A 120 J   B 7200 J   C 72 000 J   D 432 000 J

⑯ A household electricity meter reads 35 276 at 9 a.m. By 9 p.m the same day, the following appliances have been used:

a 3 kW oven for 2.5 hours;
a 2 kW dishwasher for 1 hour;
five 100 W lamps for 3 hours each;
a 2 kW tumble dryer for 30 minutes.

What is the reading on the electricity meter at 9 p.m.? *(5 marks)*

    A 35 264   B 35 288   C 36 288   D 36 777

Generating electricity and the National Grid

Generating electricity

Most electricity in Britain is generated in power stations using the energy from a non-renewable fuel. **Non-renewable fuels** take millions of years to replace. Once they are gone, they are gone forever.

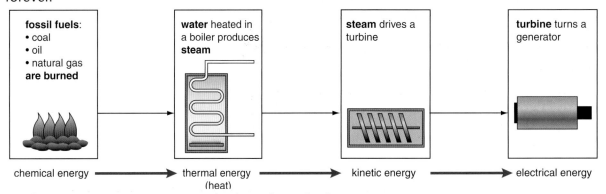

fossil fuels:	**water** heated in	**steam** drives a	**turbine** turns a
• coal	a boiler produces	turbine	generator
• oil	**steam**		
• natural gas			
are burned			

chemical energy ⟶ thermal energy (heat) ⟶ kinetic energy ⟶ electrical energy

Modern gas power stations use the heat from the burning gas to produce fast-moving air, which drives the turbine directly.

Nuclear power stations generate electricity in a similar way to those that burn coal. But the fuel is not burned in a nuclear power station. Steam is produced using the heat given out when the uranium or plutonium fuel atoms undergo **nuclear fission** reactions.

Different types of power station have different start-up times.

Start-up time is how long it takes a power station to begin to generate after it has been closed down.

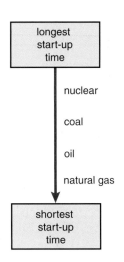

longest start-up time

nuclear

coal

oil

natural gas

shortest start-up time

The National Grid

The **National Grid** is a network of cables and transformers that transfer energy. It links the power stations that generate electricity to the consumers who use it.

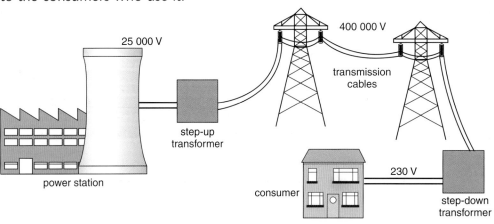

25 000 V

400 000 V

transmission cables

step-up transformer

power station

consumer

230 V

step-down transformer

■ The essential parts of the National Grid network

Transferring electrical energy at a high voltage increases efficiency

exam tip

★ You do not need to know how transformers work, only why they are used.

- The power station generates electrical energy.
- The electrical energy is transferred to a **step-up transformer**.
- The transformer increases the voltage (potential difference) across the transmission cables.
- Increasing the voltage decreases the current through the cables.
- A smaller current means less electrical energy is transformed into heat and wasted.
- Reducing the amount of waste energy makes the transfer of electrical energy more efficient.

At the end of the transmission cables, the electrical energy is transferred to a series of **step-down transformers**. These transformers decrease the voltage (potential difference) to a safe value for consumers to use.

check your understanding

17 Which type of power station is best for supplying electrical energy to the National Grid at times of peak demand? *(1 mark)*

A Nuclear   B Natural gas   C Coal   D Oil

18

Fuel	Building cost	Fuel cost	Operating cost	Decommissioning cost
Nuclear	4.2	0.4	0.6	2.7
Coal	2.0	0.3	0.7	0.1
Oil	2.2	3.5	1.2	0.1
Natural gas	2.3	1.3	0.3	0.1

The table gives an estimated cost (in pence) of generating 1 kWh of electrical energy from different fuels. Which of the following is the correct order (most expensive first) for the total cost of generating 1 kWh of electrical energy? *(1 mark)*

A natural gas, oil, coal, nuclear
B coal, natural gas, oil, nuclear
C nuclear, oil, natural gas, coal
D oil, nuclear, coal, natural gas

19 Explain how the production of electricity in a nuclear power station is different from that in a gas-burning power station. *(1 mark)*

20 It takes 5 years to build a new nuclear power station. Each year, the power used in construction is 250 MW. Once operating, the power station generates 1000 MW of power. How long will it be from the start of construction until the power station has generated more electrical energy than the energy used to build it? *(2 marks)*

Renewable energy resources

Renewable energy resources are replaced as quickly as they are used.

Most renewable energy resources used to generate electricity do not burn fuels. The energy to drive the turbine comes directly from the renewable resource.

● Energy from wind, waves and tides is freely available

The kinetic energy of wind and of moving water can be used to drive a turbine.

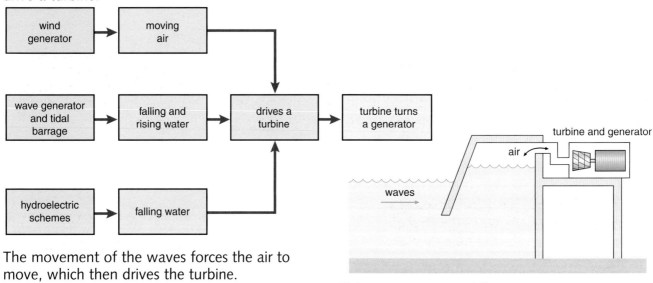

The movement of the waves forces the air to move, which then drives the turbine.

Regular tides cause the water level in an estuary to rise and fall. Turbines built into a barrage across the estuary are driven by the moving water.

■ A wave energy power station

Hydroelectric systems trap water behind a dam. The dam is built across a river to give a continuous supply of water. When released, the water falls, driving the turbines.

gravitational potential energy → kinetic energy → electrical energy

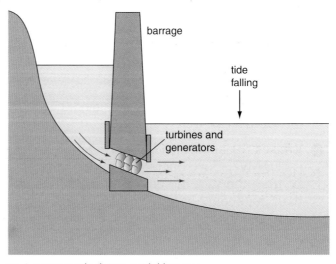

■ A generator built into a tidal barrage

A hydroelectric pumped storage power station uses surplus electricity to pump the water back up behind the dam. This makes the power station ready to generate again.

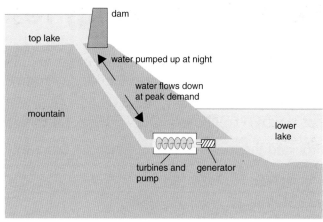

■ A pumped storage power station

Geothermal energy

In some volcanic areas, the hot rocks below the Earth's surface heat water, often turning it into steam. The steam that rises to the surface can be used to drive turbines.

Solar energy

Solar cells transform the energy of the Sun's radiation directly into electricity.

Biofuels

Biofuels come from growing plants. As they grow, they store chemical energy. Burning a biofuel transforms the chemical energy into heat, which is used to generate electricity in the same way as a coal-burning power station. Biofuels include wood, straw, olives and palm nuts.

exam tip

★ Remember to show your working in calculations. Marks may be available for each stage of the calculation.

check your understanding

㉑ What is the advantage of a tidal barrage compared with a wind generator? Select from A–D.

(1 mark)

A It has no effect on the environment.
B It generates electricity at predictable times.
C It only generates electricity when it is windy.
D It stores energy from surplus electricity.

㉒ Which type of power station involves the damming of a river? Select from A–D.   *(1 mark)*

A A wind farm.
B A wave-powered generator.
C A hydroelectric system.
D A geothermal power station.

㉓ What must be done to ensure wood is a renewable energy resource?   *(1 mark)*

㉔ Use the following information to calculate the area of solar cells needed to generate 200 kW of electrical power.

Average power from the Sun = 400 W per square metre

Efficiency of solar cells = 12.5%   *(3 marks)*

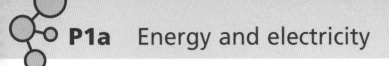

P1a Energy and electricity

Comparing energy resources

The tables below compare the advantages and disadvantages for the fuels and energy resources used to generate electricity.

⬤ Non-renewable fuels are reliable

Provided the fuel is available, electricity can always be generated.

Resource	Advantages	Disadvantages
Coal and oil	Easy to transport A concentrated source of energy	Burning releases carbon dioxide and sulfur dioxide into the air Oil has many other important uses
Natural gas	Quick to start up and to switch off	Burning releases carbon dioxide into the air
Nuclear fuels	No polluting gases produced A very concentrated source of energy – a small mass of fuel gives a huge amount of energy	Some radioactive waste must be stored for thousands of years Serious accidents may release radiation over large areas Expensive to decommission power station at the end of its useful life

Generally, renewable energy resources:

- ⬤ produce less chemical pollution than non-renewable fuels;
- ⬤ give free energy (although transforming the energy to electrical energy can be expensive).

Resource	Advantage	Disadvantage
Wind	Running costs are low Land around turbines can be used for farming	Some people think they spoil the landscape (visual pollution) and make unwanted noise Unreliable, only generate when the wind is strong enough Dilute energy resource, so a lot of turbines are needed
Waves	Running costs are low	Need to be very strong to withstand the force of a very rough sea
Tides	Reliable, the tides happen twice a day, every day	Barrages are expensive to build Barrages destroy the habitat of wading birds and other wildlife
Hydroelectric	Can be switched on and off quickly	Large areas of land may be flooded Flooding may destroy people's homes and affect plant and animal life
Solar	Ideal for remote places	Electricity generation depends on light intensity Large areas of solar cells needed to generate a lot of power
Geothermal	Massive amounts of energy available	Not always practical to extract the energy from the Earth
Biomass	Adds no additional carbon dioxide to the atmosphere	Large areas of land needed to grow the crop

Increased demand for electricity means tough decisions have to be made

The UK government wants to increase the amount of electricity generated from renewable energy resources. This could be done by erecting many more wind farms. But is this the answer? People living close to any proposed development may not want it. Balanced arguments are needed so that an informed decision can be made. A wind turbine may be the answer for people on a remote, wind-swept island, but not for those living in a new town built in a sheltered inland area.

Many governments want to reduce the emissions of carbon dioxide. In the UK, we could generate more electricity from nuclear fuels and less from fossil fuels. This would also make the UK less dependent on imported oil and gas. But how safe are nuclear power stations? And just where do you store the nuclear waste? These issues must be considered before making any decision about the future of nuclear energy.

check your understanding

25 Which reason supports the building of new nuclear power stations? *(1 mark)*

    A Nuclear waste must be stored for thousands of years.
    B Nuclear fuel is non-renewable.
    C Decommissioning costs are high.
    D A small amount of fuel generates a lot of energy.

26 The doctor in a remote African village stores medicines in a freezer. Solar cells are used to generate the electricity needed to power the freezer. The main reason for using solar cells is that: *(1 mark)*

    A Solar cells generate a constant supply of electricity.
    B The village is a long way from any other electricity supply.
    C They are safer to use than a 230 V power supply.
    D Only a small number are needed.

27 Explain why a coal-burning power station takes up less land than a wind farm that produces the same amount of electricity. *(1 mark)*

28 Why it is important to increase the amount of electricity generated using renewable energy resources? *(2 marks)*

exam tip

★ Always use the information given in a question to help you formulate arguments for or against the use of a specific energy resource.

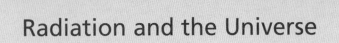

Waves and electromagnetic waves

● All waves move energy from one place to another

For example, throwing a stone into a pond causes ripples to spread out. As the water particles vibrate up and down, energy is transferred outwards from where the stone hit the water.

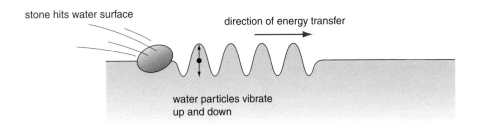

● Waves are described in terms of wavelength, frequency and amplitude

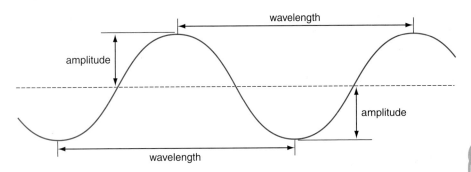

Wavelength = the distance from a point on one wave to the same point on the next wave.

Amplitude = the maximum displacement of a wave from its middle position.

Frequency = the number of waves produced each second, or the number of waves that pass a point each second.

● All waves obey the wave equation:

wave speed	=	frequency	×	wavelength
(in metres/second, m/s)		(in hertz, Hz)		(in metres, m)

exam tips

★ You don't need to remember the wave equation – but you do need to be able to rearrange it and remember the units.

★ Rearrange the equation and write it down. A mark might be given for doing this. Remember to give your answer a unit.

Electromagnetic radiation travels as waves

Electromagnetic waves form a continuous spectrum – the **electromagnetic spectrum**.

Seven types of electromagnetic wave make up the electromagnetic spectrum. The waves are grouped according to how the wavelengths are **reflected**, **absorbed** or **transmitted** by different substances and types of surface.

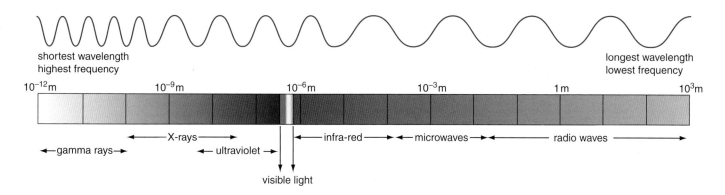

Electromagnetic waves have some common properties:

- they all travel at the same speed through a vacuum;
- they obey the wave equation;
- when absorbed, they make the absorbing material hotter;
- when absorbed by a conductor, they may produce a very small **alternating current** (a.c.) with the same **frequency** as the waves.

An alternating current is an electric current that reverses direction regularly.

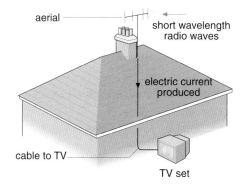

check your understanding

❶ Radio waves, used to communicate with a submarine, are transmitted through the air at a frequency of 3000 Hz. Calculate the wavelength of the waves as they travel through the air at 300 000 000 m/s. *(2 marks)*

❷ Which statement about electromagnetic waves is **not** true? *(1 mark)*

   A Radio waves travel through a vacuum at the same speed as light waves.
   B A material that absorbs electromagnetic waves gets hotter.
   C The equation wave speed = frequency × wavelength does not apply to gamma rays.
   D The frequency of an X-ray is measured in hertz.

❸ State **two** ways in which infra-red waves are different from ultraviolet waves. *(2 marks)*

❹ Which parts of the electromagnetic spectrum have a lower frequency than visible light? *(1 mark)*

Uses of electromagnetic waves

The **reflection**, **transmission** or **absorption** of an electromagnetic wave by a material or surface determines its uses.

● X-rays produce images on photographic film or computer screens

X-rays pass through low-density materials such as healthy body tissue. Denser materials, such as bone and metals, absorb X-rays. An X-ray photograph or scan shows an image of the object absorbing the X-rays.

● Microwaves and infra-red are used for cooking

Microwaves pass easily through materials such as plastic and glass, but are strongly absorbed by the water molecules inside food. The molecules gain energy, the water heats up and the food is cooked.

Warm objects **emit** infra-red; all objects **absorb** infra-red. The hot element of a toaster emits a lot of infra-red. A piece of bread absorbs the infra-red, becomes hot and is toasted.

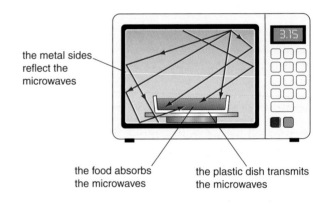

the metal sides reflect the microwaves

the food absorbs the microwaves

the plastic dish transmits the microwaves

● Visible light, infra-red, microwaves and radio waves are used for communications

Visible light and infra-red signals can be sent down an **optical fibre**. The signal travels from one end of the fibre to the other by repeated reflections. The signal even follows any curves in the fibre.

Remote controls use infra-red to carry signals over short distances.

Microwaves are used in:

● **satellite** communication systems – microwaves pass easily through the Earth's atmosphere;
● **mobile phone** networks – signals are transmitted over long distances via tall aerial masts or to another continent via a satellite.

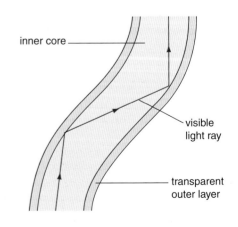

inner core

visible light ray

transparent outer layer

Radio waves are transmitted over long distances by reflecting them off the ionosphere (a layer of ionised gas in the Earth's upper atmosphere).

exam tip

★ Make sure you know why digital signals are better than analogue signals.

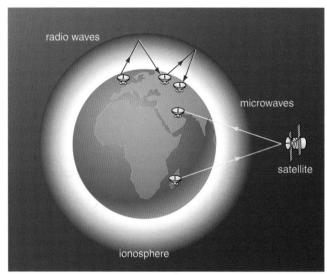

radio waves

microwaves

satellite

ionosphere

Communication signals may be analogue or digital

Analogue signals have amplitudes and frequencies that vary continuously. **Digital** signals are a coded series of 'on' and 'off' pulses. They have only two values, represented by the numbers 1 and 0.

Advantages of digital signals over analogue signals include:

- more pulses can be transmitted each second, so more information is transferred each second;
- unwanted signals (**noise**) are not recognised by a digital receiver, so the signal has a better quality (less interference);
- computers can easily **process data** sent as a digital signal.

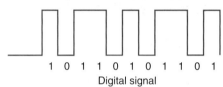

1 0 1 1 0 1 0 1 1 0 1

Digital signal

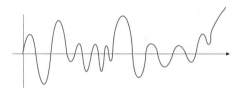

Analogue signal

check your understanding

5 Which part of the electromagnetic spectrum is used:
  a) to cook meat under a grill?
  b) in mobile phone networks?
  c) to communicate with a satelite? *(3 marks)*

6 Why are the data received by a computer less likely to be distorted by noise than the signals received by an analogue radio? *(2 marks)*

7 How can a signal, in the form of a series of light pulses, be made to follow a curved path? *(1 mark)*

8 Which one of these statements is **not** true?

  A Water molecules absorb microwaves. *(1 mark)*
  B A glass dish transmits microwaves.
  C The metal mesh inside a microwave oven door reflects microwaves.
  D Food in a microwave oven is cooked by conduction.

Hazards of electromagnetic waves

● X-rays and gamma rays are ionising radiations

Most high-frequency X-rays and gamma rays pass straight through body tissue, but some will always be **absorbed** by cells. The absorbed X-rays and gamma rays will **ionise** some atoms, which can cause changes to the molecules that control the way a cell works. This may cause gene **mutation**, damage to the central nervous system, or **cancer**.

● Different types of electromagnetic wave affect living cells in different ways

Type of wave	Effect on living cells
Gamma rays and X-rays	High doses will kill cells Low doses can cause cell mutation or cancer
Ultraviolet rays	When absorbed by the skin, the energy heats up cells and may cause sunburn The outer layers of skin may darken to give a suntan When absorbed by deeper layers of cells it may lead to skin cancer (darker skin absorbs more UV than paler skin so less UV reaches the deeper cell layers)
Infra-red rays	When absorbed by soft body tissue it is felt as heat – infra-red can cause burns
Microwaves	Living cells contain water so are heated by microwaves – this may damage or kill the cells

● Reduce the risk of cell damage by reducing exposure

X-rays – our bodies recover quickly from small doses of X-rays. So having a few X-rays taken is not hazardous. But people who operate X-ray equipment could be exposed to large doses, so often they work behind concrete or lead screens. These materials **reduce exposure** by absorbing stray X-rays.

Ultraviolet – exposure to UV causes skin cells to produce a brown pigment called melanin. This is your suntan. The darker outer layers of skin reduce the amount of UV absorbed by deeper layers of skin cells, reducing the risk of skin cancer. Sun-block creams work by reflecting or by absorbing UV, so reducing the UV absorbed by the skin.

Microwaves – mobile phone networks use microwaves. We know that, when absorbed, microwaves will **heat body cells** because the cells contain water. But at present the long-term effects of exposure to microwaves due to using a mobile phone or living near a phone mast are unknown.

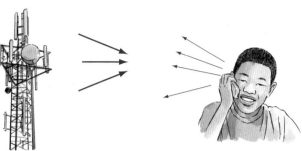

Recent research involving more than 4000 people concluded that, in the first 10 years of using a mobile phone, there was no increased risk of cancer. But **long-term risks** remain **unknown**. Experts still advise mobile phone users to reduce exposure to microwave radiation by keeping phone calls short.

exam tip

★ Something about the possible hazards of using mobile phones is a likely exam question.

check your understanding

⑨ Why is it important that scientists continue to monitor the health of mobile phone users? *(2 marks)*

⑩ Which type of electromagnetic wave is not known to cause cancer? *(1 mark)*

A microwaves   B infra-red   C gamma rays
D ultraviolet

⑪ The table gives the specific absorption rate (SAR) value for three different mobile phones. The SAR value measures the radiation energy absorbed by the head when a mobile phone is used.

Mobile phone	SAR value
X	1.41
Y	0.69
Z	0.22

SAR values are measured in the laboratory to give the maximum rate of energy absorption. The SAR value can be much lower when the phone is actually used.

a) Why is it better to give the SAR value obtained in the laboratory rather than a value obtained when the phone is in use? *(2 marks)*

b) The maximum SAR value that a phone sold in Europe can have is 2.0. Does this mean the three phones (X–Z) are safe to use? Explain the reason for your answer. *(2 marks)*

c) Some parents are going to buy a mobile phone for one of their children. Which phone, X, Y or Z, would you recommend that they buy? Explain the reason for your choice. *(2 marks)*

⑫ How does melanin help protect your skin from further damage caused by UV? *(3 marks)*

Radioactivity

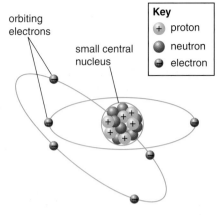

● An atom is made up of protons, neutrons and electrons

- Atoms are electrically **neutral**; they always have the same number of **protons** and **electrons**.
- All atoms of the same element have the same number of protons.
- **Isotopes** of an element have different numbers of **neutrons**.

For example, there are three isotopes of carbon as shown in the table on the right.

● Atoms of a **radioactive** substance have unstable nuclei

Radioactive substances emit radiation from the nuclei of their atoms all the time. The rate at which the substance emits radiation (**decays**) does not change, no matter what is done to the substance.

There are three types of nuclear radiation: alpha (α), beta (β) and gamma (γ):

- an **alpha** (α) particle is a helium nucleus;
- a **beta** (β) particle is an electron emitted from the nucleus of an atom;
- a **gamma** (γ) wave is a high-frequency electromagnetic wave.

The properties of these nuclear radiations are given in the table below.

To explain the effect of **electric** and **magnetic fields**:

- Only charged particles are **deflected**; gamma rays are not charged particles.
- Smaller masses are more easily deflected than larger masses; beta particles have a much smaller mass than alpha particles.
- Positive and negative charges are deflected in opposite directions; alpha particles are positive, beta particles are negative.

	Carbon-12	Carbon-13	Carbon-14
Number of protons	6	6	6
Number of neutrons	6	7	8

Radiation	Ionising power	Range in air	Penetrating power	Effect of electric and magnetic fields
Alpha (α)	Strong	A few centimetres	Absorbed by thin paper	Very small deflection
Beta (β)	Moderate	A few metres	Absorbed by a few millimetres of aluminium	Large deflection (in the opposite direction to alpha)
Gamma (γ)	Weak	A few kilometres	Absorbed by very thick lead	None

Using nuclear radiation can be dangerous

Because nuclear radiation can **ionise** atoms, it is dangerous to living cells (see page 98).

	Least dangerous	Most dangerous
Outside the body	Alpha – are easily absorbed by the air or by your skin	Gamma and beta – can penetrate the body to reach vital organs
Inside the body	Gamma and beta – can pass through cells without being absorbed	Alpha – strongly absorbed by cells and highly ionising

Ways of **reducing exposure** to nuclear radiation include:

- shielding people by using thick sheets of dense material to absorb the radiation;
- reducing the time of exposure;
- wearing protective clothing;
- handling radioactive materials remotely, or with very long tongs.

People working with radioactive substances often wear a special photographic film badge. The developed film shows the amount of radiation the person has been exposed to.

check your understanding

⓭ Which **one** of the following would not reduce the exposure of a person to the radiation emitted from a radioactive source? *(1 mark)*

   A Handling the source with long rather than short tongs.
   B Storing the source behind a concrete shield.
   C Reducing the temperature of the source.
   D Wearing a lead lined apron.

⓮ The diagram shows the paths taken through an electric field by the three different types of nuclear radiation. Which is the path of:
   a) the alpha particles?
   b) the beta particles?
   c) the gamma rays? *(3 marks)*

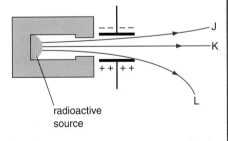

⓯ In what way are two isotopes the same, and in what way are they different? *(2 marks)*

⓰ Explain why it is important that people are not exposed to high doses of nuclear radiation. *(2 marks)*

Uses of radioactivity

● Radioactive decay is a random process

It's impossible to predict when one unstable nucleus will decay. But with a large group of unstable atoms, we can estimate how many nuclei will decay in a period of time. The decay of a large group of unstable atoms always follows the same pattern.

The average number of emissions in a certain time is called the **count rate**.

- ● The time it takes for the count rate or the number of nuclei of a radioactive isotope to fall to half its initial value is called the **half-life**.
- ● The shorter the half-life, the faster the isotope decays and the more unstable it is.

Radioactive wastes often have long half-lives. This means they decay slowly and will be around for a long time. Hence the problem we have in storing some types of radioactive waste for thousands of years.

● The use of an isotope depends on its half-life and on the type of radiation emitted

Medical tracers have a short half-life and usually emit gamma radiation. A medical **tracer** is a radioactive isotope attached to a chemical, then injected into a patient. The gamma rays (or sometimes beta particles) emitted are detected outside the patient's body. A short half-life (but long enough for doctors to carry out a diagnosis) means the level of radiation inside the patient's body soon falls to a safe level. Technetium-99 is often used as a medical tracer.

Tracers also have many industrial applications, including:

- ● locating leaks in underground pipes;
- ● finding the source of river pollution;
- ● **Gamma rays are used to sterilise food and medical instruments**.

Gamma rays kill bacteria – so gamma radiation can be used to:

- ● **sterilise** medical instruments and dressings;
- ● keep food fresh for longer (the food does not become radioactive!).

Cobalt-60 is often used to kill bacteria. The long half-life means the source does not need changing too often.

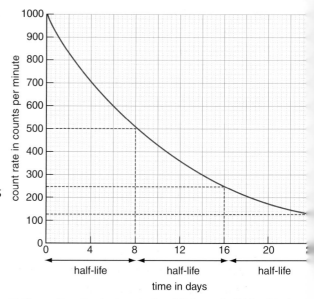

■ The radioactive isotope iodine-131 has a half-life of 8 days

exam tips

- ★ You need to be able to find the half-life from a graph like this.
- ★ Make sure you look at the units on axes; time could be in seconds, minutes, days or years.

Isotope	Useful radiation emitted	Half-life
Cobalt-60	Gamma	5.3 years
Technetium-99	Gamma	6 hours
Phosphorus-32	Beta	14 days
Manganese-52	Gamma	5.6 days
Strontium-90	Beta	28 years
Radon-220	Alpha	52 seconds

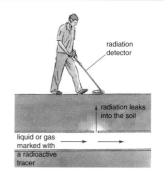

Isotopes used for quality control often have a long half-life. A thick sheet of material will absorb more radiation than a thin sheet of material. So measuring the level of radiation passing through the sheet will monitor the thickness as the sheet is being produced. The control unit responds to the radiation detected, automatically adjusting the pressure the rollers exert on the sheet.

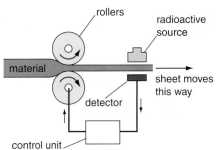

- For materials such as paper, cardboard and plastic, a beta source is used.
- For a metal sheet, a gamma source is used as it has greater penetrating power.

check your understanding

⑰ Look at the list of isotopes in the table opposite. Which isotope would be used in the following situations? Explain the reason for each choice. *(6 marks)*
   a) To monitor the thickness of polythene as it is produced.
   b) To kill the cells in a cancerous tumour.
   c) To trace the path of oil in an underground pipe.

exam tip

★ You must consider both the type of radiation emitted and the half-life.

⑱ A radioactive isotope contains 128 000 undecayed nuclei. After 16 days, this number has gone down to 8000. Calculate the half-life of the isotope. *(2 marks)*

⑲ The number of radioactive emissions from a source in a given time is called: *(1 mark)*

   A half-life.   B count rate.   C rate of reaction.   D decay constant.

⑳ The graphs below show how three different radioactive isotopes decay with time. Which isotope has:
   a) the shortest half-life?
   b) the slowest rate of decay?
   c) the highest percentage of undecayed nuclei remaining after 10 years?
   d) the possibility of being used as a medical tracer? *(4 marks)*

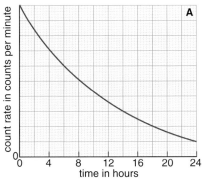
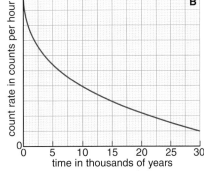
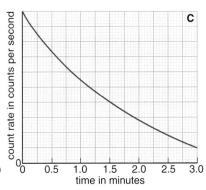

Stars and telescopes

● Telescopes are used to observe the Solar System and the galaxies in the Universe

Stars emit visible light and other electromagnetic radiation such as radio waves or X-rays. Various types of telescope detect electromagnetic radiation from space.

Optical telescopes detect visible light, producing **magnified** images that we can see with our eyes. These telescopes are often built on **high mountains** where the atmosphere is thinner. The thinner the atmosphere, the less it **distorts** the light from a star or galaxy, so the clearer the image will be. Weather conditions also affect the quality of the image – clouds block light.

Weak radio signals given off by very distant stars and galaxies can pass through the atmosphere. The signals received by several **radio telescopes** are often processed by computers to produce an image of the stars and galaxies emitting the signals.

Other types of telescope detect gamma rays, X-rays, ultraviolet (UV) or infra-red.

■ Telescopes are placed on mountain-tops as the layer of atmosphere above the telescope is thinner

Some telescopes are mounted on satellites in orbit around the Earth.

Different **space telescopes** detect different types of electromagnetic radiation. The Hubble Space Telescope detects infra-red, visible light and UV radiation.

Telescope	Advantages	Disadvantages
Earth-based telescope	Easy to maintain Telescopes can be linked to give greater detail	Need huge structures to support and move the mirror Images distorted by the atmosphere Light absorbed by clouds
Space telescope	Images not distorted by the atmosphere Signals not affected by the weather More sensitive to weaker signals Can measure smaller and more distant objects in space	Very expensive to build and put into orbit Difficult to maintain

check your understanding

㉑ What are the advantages of a space telescope over a telescope on Earth?   *(2 marks)*

㉒ Why are Earth-based telescopes often built on high mountains?   *(1 mark)*

Expanding Universe and 'big bang'

● The 'big bang' theory predicts that the Universe is expanding

The **'big bang' theory** suggests that the Universe began with a huge explosion, billions of years ago. At that moment, all the matter in the Universe, concentrated at a tiny point in space, started to expand outwards into the Universe we have today. This is only a theory – scientists cannot prove the theory, but they can look for evidence to support it.

● What is red-shift?

Red-shift is an example of the **Doppler effect**.

The Doppler effect happens with all waves, but is most easily noticed with **sound**. If a sound of constant pitch moves away from you, the pitch of the sound you hear decreases. This happens because the wavelength of the waves increases – an example of the Doppler effect.

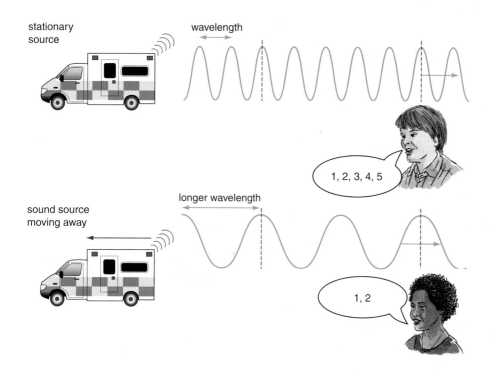

If a light source moved away from you quickly enough, the light waves you see would also have a longer wavelength. This would make the light appear as if it has moved to the red end of the spectrum. The light would show a red-shift.

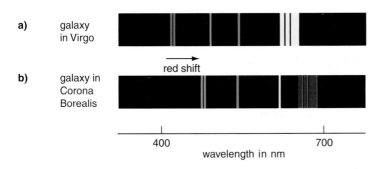

a) galaxy in Virgo

red shift

b) galaxy in Corona Borealis

400   700
wavelength in nm

● Red-shift provides evidence for a rapidly expanding Universe

When scientists look at the light from distant **galaxies**, it shows a red-shift. So the galaxies must be **moving away** from the Earth at great speed. Scientists have observed that the further a galaxy is from the Earth, the bigger the red-shift. This observation can be explained by suggesting that galaxies further away must be moving more quickly.

So, at some time in the past they must have been closer together. Red-shift provides evidence to support the 'big bang' theory.

The 'big bang' theory is not the only way of explaining how the Universe began. Currently it is the most popular – but ideas can change. New evidence, once shown to be reliable, may mean adapting or even discarding the 'big bang' theory. A theory is only as good as the evidence that supports it.

check your understanding

㉓ What evidence is there to support the 'big bang' theory?
(3 marks)

㉔ Which one of the following statements about the 'big bang' theory is correct? *(1 mark)*

  A It is the only way of explaining the origin of the Universe.
  B There is scientific evidence to support the theory.
  C It is based on scientific and religious facts.
  D Scientists have proof that it happened.

exam tip

★ A popular exam question – you should be able to write down three points.

Answers

B1a

Nervous system and reflexes

1 a) Touch, pressure, light, sound, taste/chemicals/smell, temperature, changes in position. *(7 marks)*

b) Sensory nerves take nerve impulses into the spinal cord; motor nerves take nerve impulses away from the spinal cord. *(2 marks)*

2 Sense organ; receptor cells; sensory nerves; motor nerves; effectors. *(1 mark each)*

Hormones, the menstrual cycle and fertility

3 Pituitary; ovaries; oestrogen; luteinising hormone. *(1 mark each)*

4 a) At ovulation/day 14. *(1 mark)*

b) Levels vary throughout the month so a low reading could just correspond to the part of the cycle when levels are low; best to time the measurement when the level should be highest. *(2 marks)*

Controlling internal conditions

5 a) Increased sweating; increased breathing rate so more water lost from the mouth. *(2 marks)*

b) Sweat contains both water and ions. *(1 mark)*

c) Hot climate; accept diarrhoea. *(1 mark)*

6 B *(1 mark)*

Drugs: good and bad

7 Side effects, human tissue, live animals, clinical trials. *(1 mark each)*

8 a) Feel happy; **b)** brain stops producing the hormone naturally; **c)** unhappy; **d)** being dependent on the drug, not being able to function without it; **e)** when they stop taking the drug they get withdrawal symptoms, which means they need to take more to function again. *(5 marks)*

Tobacco and cannabis

9 D *(1 mark)*

10 a) Nicotine *(1 mark)* is addictive *(1 mark)*.

b) Better treatment available *(1 mark)*, earlier diagnosis *(1 mark)*.

c) Less chance of low birth-weight babies

11 The correlation *(1 mark)* may be due to chance or other causes *(1 mark)*; in this case a linking factor is long sunny days *(1 mark)*.

Diet and exercise

12 Energy requirements, glucose, metabolic rate. *(1 mark each)*

13 C *(1 mark)*

14 a) 29 minutes; **b)** 200 minutes. *(2 marks)*

Problems with 'bad' diets

15 Obesity, high cholesterol, smoking, genetics, high fat diet, stress. *(2 marks)*

16 Obese, saturated fat, heart disease, statins, side effects. *(1 mark each)*

Fighting disease

17 Produce antibodies, produce antitoxins, ingest microorganisms *(3 marks)*

18 C *(1 mark)*

The fight against disease – then and now

19 To reduce the rate *(1 mark)* at which antibiotic-resistant bacteria *(1 mark)* develop.

20 Semmelweiss's idea that microorganisms are transferred by contact/touch *(1 mark)*, need for very good hygiene in hospitals to stop spread of infections *(1 mark)*.

21 B *(1 mark)*

B1b

Adapt and survive

1 Toxins, spines, bright colouration, armour etc. *(1 mark for each)*

2 C *(1 mark)*

Populations and competition

3 a) Habitat destruction, hunters, egg collectors, pollution. *(1 mark)*

b) Protection of habitat, re-introduction into wild, more food, less pollution. *(2 marks)*

4 A *(1 mark)*

Variation and inheritance

5 a) Twins are usually brought up in the same environment (e.g. in the same house, by

the same parents) *(1 mark)*, which is not true for any two other children *(1 mark)*.
b) Very small sample, to invalid. *(1 mark)*
⑥ B *(1 mark)*

Reproduction and cloning

⑦ Adult cell cloning produces an identical copy of a particular individual (i.e. one that already exists) *(1 mark)*. Embryo transfer makes multiple copies of an individual that has never existed before (i.e. a new baby) *(1 mark)*.
⑧ C *(1 mark)*

Genetic engineering

⑨ Can apply weedkiller over a whole field and not worry about killing the crops. *(1 mark)*
⑩ C *(1 mark)*

The fossil record

⑪ D *(1 mark)*

How evolution happens

⑫ Any example of a skill or characteristic acquired by a parent that is not passed to offspring (e.g. learning Chinese, bodybuilder's large muscles, losing a limb in an accident). *(1 mark)*
⑬ Either: in Darwin's theory the variation is present from birth but in Lamarck's theory the characteristic changes when the environment changes; or in Lamarck's theory evolution happens to individuals but in Darwin's theory populations are important. *(2 marks)*

How do humans affect the environment?

⑭ **a)** One near where cars go, one away from cars; more air pollution less lichen. *(2 marks)*
b) Random number generator *(1 mark)*
c) There could be random variations over the site so one sample would not be representative *(1 mark)*; improve reliability of data *(1 mark)*.
⑮ Acid rain, global warming, sewage, deforestation. *(4 marks)*

Global warming

⑯ More cattle; more rice cultivation. *(2 marks)*
⑰ Concentration increases *(1 mark)*, as there

are fewer trees to remove carbon dioxide from the atmosphere *(1 mark)*. (Note: burning is not mentioned in the question so cannot say more carbon dioxide is released.)
⑱ D *(1 mark)*

Sustainable development

⑲ Recycling paper means fewer forests are cut down; recycling glass and metals means that fewer quarries are dug. *(2 marks)*
⑳ C *(1 mark)*

C1a

Atoms, elements and the Periodic Table

① As on page 40. *(3 marks)*
② An element – it is made of only one sort of atom. *(1 mark)*
③ C *(1 mark)*
④ C *(1 mark)*

Reactions, formulae and balanced equations

⑤ A, electrons. *(1 mark)*
⑥ hydrogen + oxygen → water *(2 marks)*
⑦ $2H_2 + O_2 \rightarrow 2H_2O$ *(2 marks)*
⑧ **a)** $CH_4 + 2O_2 \rightarrow CO_2 + 2H_2O$ *(2 marks)*
b) $2Na + 2H_2O \rightarrow H_2 + 2NaOH$ *(2 marks)*
c) $H_2SO_4 + 2NaOH \rightarrow Na_2SO_4 + 2H_2O$ *(2 marks)*

Products from limestone

⑨ copper carbonate → copper oxide + carbon dioxide
$$CuCO_3 \quad \rightarrow \quad CuO \quad + \quad CO_2$$
(3 marks)
⑩ water + calcium oxide → calcium hydroxide
$$H_2O + \quad CaO \quad \rightarrow \quad Ca(OH)_2$$
(4 marks)
⑪ C *(1 mark)*

Extracting metals

⑫ The least reactive metals, such as gold, platinum and silver, are found as themselves. *(1 mark)*
⑬ Reduction. *(1 mark)*
⑭ A *(1 mark)*

Quarrying, mining and recycling

⑮ Three advantages of living close to a quarry: the quarry provides jobs; new road links are built; the company provides some social benefits. *(3 marks)*

16 Three disadvantages of living close to a quarry: it is ugly while it is being dug; there is more noise pollution than before; wildlife habitats are destroyed. *(3 marks)*

17 C *(1 mark)*

Using metals and alloys

18 Impurities *(1 mark)* make it brittle *(1 mark)*.

19 They return to their original shape after being deformed. *(1 mark)*

20 C *(1 mark)*

21 A *(1 mark)*

Crude oil

22 D *(1 mark)*

23 Numbers of carbon atoms in them (and therefore similar boiling points). *(2 marks)*

24 B *(1 mark)*

25 Boiling point *(1 mark)* increases with molecule size *(1 mark)*; viscosity *(1 mark)* increases with molecule size. *(1 mark)*

Burning fuels

26 $C_5H_{12} + 8O_2 \rightarrow 5CO_2 + 6H_2O$ *(2 marks)*

27 Carbon dioxide *(1 mark)* increases temperature (global warming) *(1 mark)* but soot *(1 mark)* decreases temperature (global dimming) *(1 mark)*.

28 D *(1 mark)*

29 A *(1 mark)*

Cleaner fuels

30 Reducing sulfur in petrol; removing sulphur from gases at a power station (flue gas desulfurisation). *(2 marks)*

31 Advantages: renewable (do not use up non-renewable fuels); clean (no pollutants when burnt). Disadvantages: takes a lot of land to grow; less energy output. *(4 marks)*

32 **a)** ethanol + oxygen → carbon dioxide + water *(2 marks)*
   b) $C_2H_5OH + 3O_2 \rightarrow 2CO_2 + 3H_2O$ *(2 marks)*

33 C *(1 mark)*

C1b

Cracking crude oil

1 C *(2 marks)*

2 D *(1 mark)*

3 Margarine will react with iodine solution to change it from brown or purple to colourless. *(2 marks)*

4 As on page 58 *(2 marks)*

Making ethanol

5 Because ethanol has a lower *(1 mark)* boiling point *(1 mark)* than the rest of the mixture.

6 A *(1 mark)*

7 C *(1 mark)*

Making polymers

8 Poly(propene). *(1 mark)*

9 Alkenes, monomers, large, ethene. *(1 mark each)*

10 C *(1 mark)*

Waste disposal problems

11 B *(1 mark)*

12 *Any six valid points, but must score 4 (1 per box) first.*

	Advantages	Disadvantages
Crude oil products as fuels	High energy output Easy to produce	Produce pollution Uses finite resource only once
Crude oil products as raw materials	Can make lots of use of the oil Many products Many uses	Reduces availability for fuel

Vegetable oils and fuels

13 **a)** Contains carbon–carbon double bonds. *(1 mark)*
   b) Melt *(1 mark)*, add iodine water or bromine water *(1 mark)*.
   c) Less risk of heart disease and strokes *(1 mark)* due to less cholesterol *(1 mark)*.
   d) React them with hydrogen *(1 mark)* in the presence of a nickel catalyst *(1 mark)* at about 60 °C *(1 mark)*.

14 Crops (such as sugar cane). *(1 mark)*

15 D *(1 mark)*

16 D *(1 mark)*

Food additives and emulsifiers

17 A *(1 mark)*

18 A *(1 mark)*

19 B *(1 mark)*

The Earth and continental drift

⑳ As on page 70. *(4 marks)*
㉑ A new scientific theory becomes accepted by other scientists as they check each other's ideas and evidence. *(1 mark for checking, 1 mark for each other)*
㉒ C *(1 mark)*
㉓ B *(1 mark)*

Plate tectonics

㉔ A *(1 mark)*
㉕ B *(1 mark)*
㉖ Earthquakes occur at the boundaries between tectonic plates *(1 mark)* as the result of sudden movement. *(1 mark)*

Gases in the atmosphere

㉗ **a)** 32% *(2 marks)*
   b) More carbon dioxide from burning fuels; increase in industrialisation. *(2 marks)*
㉘ D *(1 mark)*
㉙ C *(1 mark)*

Theories about the atmosphere

㉚ Oxygen increased *(1 mark)* from nearly zero *(1 mark)*; carbon dioxide decreased *(1 mark)* from very high level to almost zero *(1 mark)*.
㉛ These processes acted over hundreds of millions of years *(1 mark)*; we have only a century or less *(1 mark)*.
㉜ C *(1 mark)*

Answers

P1a

Thermal radiation

① The hot pie is at a higher temperature than the refrigerator; the hot pie emits thermal radiation at a faster rate than it absorbs thermal radiation (or it emits thermal radiation to the surroundings). *(2 marks)*
② **a)** A matt white, B shiny black, C matt black, D shiny silver *(4 marks)*
   b) So the small differences in emitted thermal radiation can be measured. *(1 mark)*
③ **a)** Y, the room is at a constant temperature. *(2 marks)*
   b) 22 °C. *(2 marks)*

Conduction and convection

④ At the top of the box. Cold air is denser than warm air, so will fall through the box, keeping the contents cool. *(3 marks)*
⑤ C and E *(2 marks)*
⑥ Copper contains mobile electrons, plastic does not. *(1 mark)*

Reducing rates of heat (thermal energy) transfer

⑦ A black surface is a good absorber of thermal radiation; copper is a good conductor of thermal radiation; aluminium foil reflects thermal radiation back towards the water pipes; expanded foam contains small pockets of air, which is a good insulator so reducing the thermal energy loss. *(6 marks)*
⑧ The wool traps pockets of air and air is a good insulator. *(2 marks)*
⑨ **a)** No – the reduction in energy loss and small savings in energy bills does not justify the additional cost (has a long payback time); or yes – any reduction in energy loss is worthwhile (despite the additional cost). *(1 mark)*
   b) The figures would increase – heat transfer increases with temperature difference. *(2 marks)*
   c) 1 and 3; or 2 and 4 *(1 mark)*

Energy efficiency

⑩ £39.40 *(3 marks)*
⑪ C *(1 mark)*
⑫ **a)** 800 J *(2 marks)*
   b) Switching off the energy input is zero or energy is still wasted. *(1 mark)*
⑬ B *(2 marks)*

Electrical power and energy costs

⑭ £18 *(4 marks)*
⑮ D *(2 marks)*
⑯ B *(5 marks)*

Generating electricity and the National Grid

⑰ B *(1 mark)*
⑱ C *(1 mark)*
⑲ Nuclear fuel is not burned. *(1 mark)*
⑳ 6 years 3 months (accept 7 years) *(2 marks)*

Renewable energy resources

㉑ B *(1 mark)*
㉒ C *(1 mark)*
㉓ Replant at same rate as it is harvested (cut down). *(1 mark)*
㉔ $4000\,m^2$ *(3 marks)*

Comparing energy resources

㉕ D *(1 mark)*
㉖ B *(1 mark)*
㉗ Coal is a concentrated energy resource *or* wind is a dilute energy resource. *(1 mark)*
㉘ Reasons could include: to conserve fossil fuels; to reduce air pollution; to cope with increasing demand. *(2 marks)*

P1b

Waves and electromagnetic waves

① $100\,000\,m$ (100 km) *(2 marks)*
② C *(1 mark)*
③ Infra-red waves have a longer wavelength and lower frequency. *(2 marks)*
④ Microwaves, radio waves, infra-red *(1 mark)*

Uses of electromagnetic waves

⑤ **a)** Infra-red; **b)** microwaves; **c)** microwaves *(3 marks)*
⑥ Data are received by a computer as digital signals; noise is not recognised by a digital receiver but distorts an analogue signal. *(2 marks)*
⑦ Transmit through an optical fibre. *(1 mark)*
⑧ D *(1 mark)*

Hazards of electromagnetic waves

⑨ Evidence relating mobile phone use to health is limited to the first 10 years of use; the long-term effect on health in unknown. *(2 marks)*
⑩ B infra-red *(1 mark)*
⑪ **a)** So you know the maximum exposure *or,* if tested under the same conditions, different phones can be compared. *(2 marks)*
   b) No, there is no proof that absorbing even small amounts of radiation energy is totally harmless. *(2 marks)*
   c) Z, the amount of radiation absorbed is the lowest so you can expect it to present the least hazard. *(2 marks)*

⑫ Causes the outer layers of skin to darken; the darker the skin, the more UV is absorbed so less UV penetrates to reach deeper layers of skin. *(3 marks)*

Radioactivity

⑬ C *(1 mark)*
⑭ **a)** Alpha, J; **b)** beta, L; **c)** gamma, K *(3 marks)*
⑮ Have same number of protons (and electrons); have different numbers of neutrons. *(2 marks)*
⑯ Can ionise the atoms of living cells, causing damage to the cells or cancer. *(2 marks)*

Uses of radioactivity

⑰ **a)** Strontium-90, level of beta radiation detected changes with thickness of polythene; gamma radiation would be unchanged, alpha would be stopped; long half-life so source does not need changing often.
   b) Cobalt-60, gamma rays pass through the body to the tumour; radiation can kill cells; long half-life so source does not need to be replaced too often.
   c) Manganese-52, gamma rays pass through the ground to be detected; long enough half-life to take measurements, but not so long that oil becomes contaminated. *(6 marks)*
⑱ 4 days *(2 marks)*
⑲ B *(1 mark)*
⑳ **a)** C; **b)** B **c)** B; **d)** A *(4 marks)*

Stars and telescopes

㉑ Images are not distorted by the atmosphere or affected by the weather; more sensitive to weaker signals, so can measure smaller and more distant objects in space. *(2 marks)*
㉒ Atmosphere produces less image distortion. *(1 mark)*

Expanding Universe and 'big bang'

㉓ Light from distant galaxies shows a red-shift, so galaxies are moving away from the Earth and Universe is expanding as predicted by the 'big bang' theory. *(3 marks)*
㉔ B *(1 mark)*

Index

Index

nerves   2, 3
neurones   2
neutron   100
nicotine   10
noble gases   74
noise in signals   97
non-biodegradable   64
non-renewable   34, 38, 56, 88
nuclear fission   88
nuclear power   88, 92
nuclear radiation 100, 101
nucleus   25, 40

obesity   14, 67
oestrogen   5
opinions, evaluating   11, 48, 55
optical fibre   97
ores   46
ovaries   4
overweight   13, 14
ovulation   4

painkiller   16
pancreas   6
pandemic   18
particles from combustion   54, 60
pathogens   16, 22
payback time   85
Periodic Table   41
pesticide   34
photosynthesis   36, 77
pituitary gland   4
placebo   9
plastics   58, 62
plate tectonics   72
pollution   23, 34, 38, 92
poly(chloroethene)   62
poly(ethene)   62
poly(propene)   62
polymers   62, 65
polymers, disposal   64
population growth   34
potential difference   89
power   86
power stations   88, 92
power transmission   89
precision of measurements   79
predator   22, 30
preservatives   68
prey   22
processed food   15
protein   12
proton   100
PVC   62

quadrat   35
quarrying   44, 48
quicklime   44

radiation from radioactive substances   100, 101
radiation of heat energy   78, 82
radiators   81
radio telescopes   104
radio waves   95, 97
radioactive decay   100
radioactive waste   92, 102
radioactivity   100
radioactivity, uses of   102
random error   79
random sample   35
reaction time   8
reactivity series   46
receptor cells   2, 6
recycling   38, 49, 64
red-shift   106
reduction   46
reflect   78, 95, 96, 97
reflex   3
relay neurones   3
reliable data   7, 9, 15, 78
renewable energy resources 67, 90, 92
repeated measurements   78
representative sample   35
resources, limited 22, 49
respiration   13

salt   14, 15
sample size   10, 15
sampling technique   35
satellite communication   97
saturated fat   15, 66, 67
saturated hydrocarbons   52
sea level rise   37
Semmelweiss, Ignaz   18
sense organs   2
sensitivity of measurements   79
sensory neurones   3
sewage   34
sexual reproduction   26
shape-memory alloys   51
shape-memory polymers   62
shiny surfaces   78, 83
side-effects 9
skin cancer   98
slaked lime   44
slime   62
slimming   12

smart alloys   51
smart materials   44
smart polymers   62
smoking   10, 11
solar cells   91, 93
soot   54
sperm   26
sports drinks   7
stainless steel   50
stars   104
start-up time   89, 92
statins   15
steel   50
stimulus   2
sulfur dioxide   34, 54, 56
surface area-to-volume ratio   20
surveys   10, 15
survival advantage   32
sustainable development   38
synapse   3
systematic error   35

tar   10
target cells   4
tectonic plates   72
telescope   104
temperature control in body   6
temperature, measuring   78
thalidomide   9
thermal decomposition   45, 58
thermal radiation   78
thermoplastic   62
thermosetting   62
thorns   20, 21
tidal power   90, 93
tissue culture   27
titanium, uses   51
tobacco   10
toxins   16
tracers   102
transferring energy   84
transformer   89
transforming energy   84
transition metals   50
transmit (radiation)   95, 96
transmitter chemicals   3
turbine   88
twins   26

ultraviolet radiation   98
Universe, expansion of   106
unsaturated fats   15
unsaturated hydrocarbons   58
unsaturated oils   66

Index